D1044819

AURAS

First published in 2020 by Wellfleet Press,
an imprint of The Quarto Group
142 West 36th Street, 4th Floor
New York, NY 10018, USA
T (212) 779-4972 F (212) 779-6058
www.QuartoKnows.com

10 9 8 7 6 5 4 3 2 1

ISBN: 978-1-57715-224-8

Library of Congress Control Number: 2020942716

Publisher: Rage Kindelsperger
Creative Director: Laura Drew
Managing Editor: Cara Donaldson
Senior Editor: John Foster
Cover and Interior Design: Ashley Prine, Tandem Books

Printed in China

IN FOCUS

AURAS

Your Personal Guide

Joylina Goodings

WELLFLEET PRESS

CONTENTS

INTRODUCTION

WHAT IS AN AURA?

Everything in the universe is made up of energy, and that energy emits an energy field around it. This includes not only us but animals, trees, plants, insects, mountains, hills, rocks, planets, stars, and so on. This energy field surrounding all living things is known as an *aura*, and in most cases, it is invisible but there are some things that radiate an aura that are easy to see. For example, we can often see the aura around our moon and the sun as a faint shimmering energy radiating out of them. Auras can be photographed using special cameras, but with practice, you can learn to see, sense, and feel this energy field with just the naked eye. Exercises later in this book will help you hone these skills, which focus on our own auras, that is, the human aura.

The word *aura* comes from the Greek word meaning "air" or "breeze." It's the pure life-force energy that in Chinese is known as *chi*, in Japanese as *qi*, in Hawaiian as *mana*, and in Sanskrit, within the Indian Buddhist tradition, as *prana*, where it is often depicted as a thousand-petal lotus flower enshrining the head of Buddha as well as all those who reach enlightenment.

Auras surround all things and interact with all things. A human aura is made up of electromagnetic particles that radiate from the body. It holds all the positive and negative information from our past, our present, and our near future. It's our life-force energy, and from this energy, a sensitive person can pick up on everything about us—physically, mentally, emotionally, and spiritually—because our auras reflect our ever-changing moods as well as our physical, emotional, and spiritual health.

This means the personal aura surrounding you not only holds all the information about you, it's also influenced by your surroundings and the living beings that are in your vicinity whom you're interacting with. This of course means that not only do others' auras influence you, but your aura influences others as well.

You are probably aware that some places and some people "feel" good and others do not. Some are welcoming, some are not. Animals such as dogs are particularly sensitive to a person's aura. They know if someone they meet likes them or is frightened, and they behave accordingly. We all take instant likes and dislikes to others, and we don't know why. The reason is that we are unconsciously sensing another's aura and the energy within it. For instance, we often sense someone is upset or angry, regardless of the smile on their face. We ask them how they are, and they reply "fine" and we "know" they are lying. If we know them well, we may persist in our questions, but if we are meeting someone for the first time, we probably won't trust them. Our auras are constantly changing and reflecting our ever-shifting moods and feelings as well as interacting with the differing energies that surround everything—ourselves included.

The objectives of this book are to teach you about your own, how your aura interacts with those of others, and how that interaction then affects your own energy and moods. You will discover tools and techniques you can use to invigorate your aura and raise your energy when you are tired. You will find new ways in which to expand your sensitivity and intuition so that you can lead a happier and healthier life by maintaining a healthy aura and understanding the auras of those around you. You will see how when the mind, the body, and the spirit are in alignment, the aura is fresh and bright, and when they are out of balance—whether through accident, illness, or emotional or mental trauma—how they can become blocked. You will discover how to identify and release these blockages, because where the blockages, also called *smudges*, are within the aura reflects back to us the underlying unconscious cause. Thus, the aura itself can enlighten us as to what we need to do to become balanced and whole so as to come back in line with the successful lives we were all born to live.

You will also learn how the energy of others affects our energy because of the interaction of the auras. You will find out how to help yourself and others with tools such as colors, crystals, essential oils, sounds, and healing energies, such as reiki or spiritual healing, to refresh, heal, and balance not only your own aura but also those of others.

Enclosed Aura Wall Chart

Included in this book is a wall chart that serves as a quick and handy reference guide to the essential information on auras found on the following pages.

❋ ❋ ❋

1

THE HISTORY OF AURA AWARENESS

References to the aura can be traced back not only to the glowing halos of spiritual energy used by artists portraying Jesus and the saints, but also to even earlier religious traditions. Energy as the basis of life was a major part of ancient Egyptian religion and art, and similar beliefs were held by ancient Greeks as well as people throughout the Asian continent.

Many people wrote of light radiating from humans, animals, and holy places, with the most famous being Pythagoras (born 570 BCE). In the modern world he may be best known for his contribution to mathematics, but in his own time he was known as a mystical teacher who taught of the light energy around all beings—i.e., auras. Joan of Arc (c. 1412–1431) is probably the best known of the Christian mystics who wrote about divine light, while both testaments of the Bible are full of references to "divine light" and "the light of God." Saint Teresa of Ávila (1515–1582) wrote about her mystical experiences, which included hearing voices and seeing visions of light.

In more recent times, any mention of visions or of seeing light and color around people was enough to have you incarcerated in a mental institution. Only sensitive people such as healers and clairvoyants would admit to it, and in most cases they were considered crazy or fraudulent.

Over the years, technology has been able to photograph and measure these energy fields. With the development of ever more sensitive technology, we can video the interaction of people's auras when they meet and the reaction to people's aura's while receiving healing and vibrational medicine. This can all now be objectively measured and studied. The first images were created by Nikola Tesla in 1891, although like a lot of Tesla's work, it was ignored until more recently.

Pythagoras

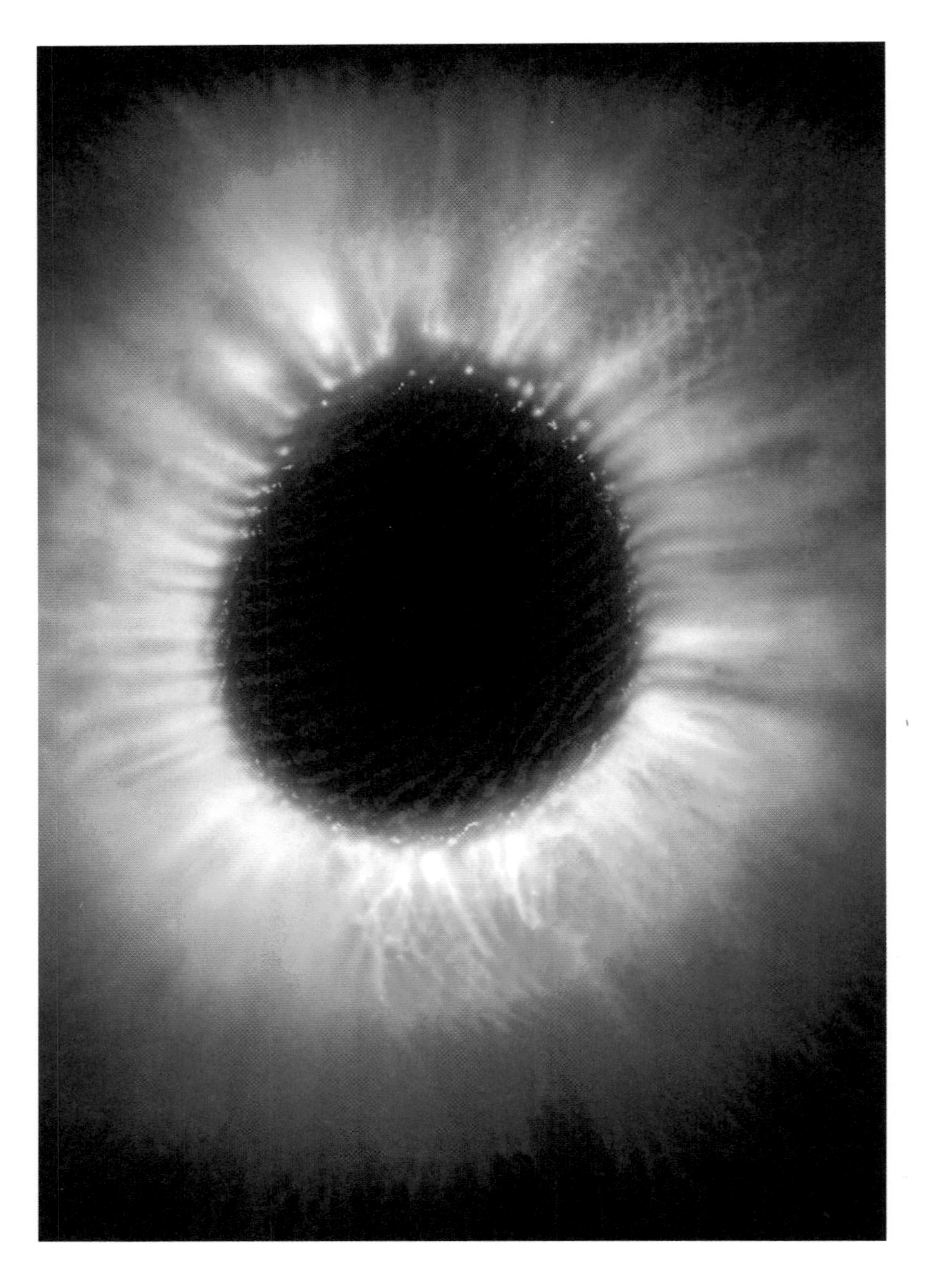

Kirlian Photograph of a Fingertip

EEGs (electroencephalograms) measure magnetic impulses and tiny electrical currents in the brain, while polygraphs (lie detectors) measure the fluctuations of electrical impulses that result from changes in our emotions. Semyon Kirlian invented Kirlian photography, which captures these electrical fluctuations and transfers them onto film. His photography became known around the world in the early 1960s for capturing the results that take place when a person or animal responds to changes within their physical, mental, or emotional states.

By 1975, human auras were being researched in universities around the world, revealing that energy fields surrounded not just people and animals, but also trees, rocks, mountains, and just about everything around us. Research also showed that an aura's energy is concentrated within hundreds of specific areas of the body. These areas appear to correlate to the acupuncture points within the Chinese meridian system of healing as well as the seven main chakras that pass through the center of the body within the Indian chakra system. It appeared that an aura's energy centers confirmed what doctors of Chinese and Indian medicine had known for centuries.

Since then many different types of aura cameras have been developed for research purposes. They show all or part of the aura, especially the colors of the aura. So much has been learned over the years, including how an aura changes due to both internal and external influences—when a person thinks of different things, either positive or negative, for example. This creates an emotion within the body that is then reflected in the aura. When we are thinking things that make us sad, for example, the aura will lack luster and will probably show a lot of blue—but more of that later.

People automatically connect and intuit information like this from auras. For most of us, it's unconscious for example; you get a "feeling" about a place or person upon which you base your opinion. However, the more you learn and the more you can access the information in auras, the more you're able to help yourself, family, friends, and even the world.

As we progress through this book, you will learn how being able to connect to and read auras allows you to heal yourself, others, and our greater environment, thus enabling you to live a richly fulfilling life.

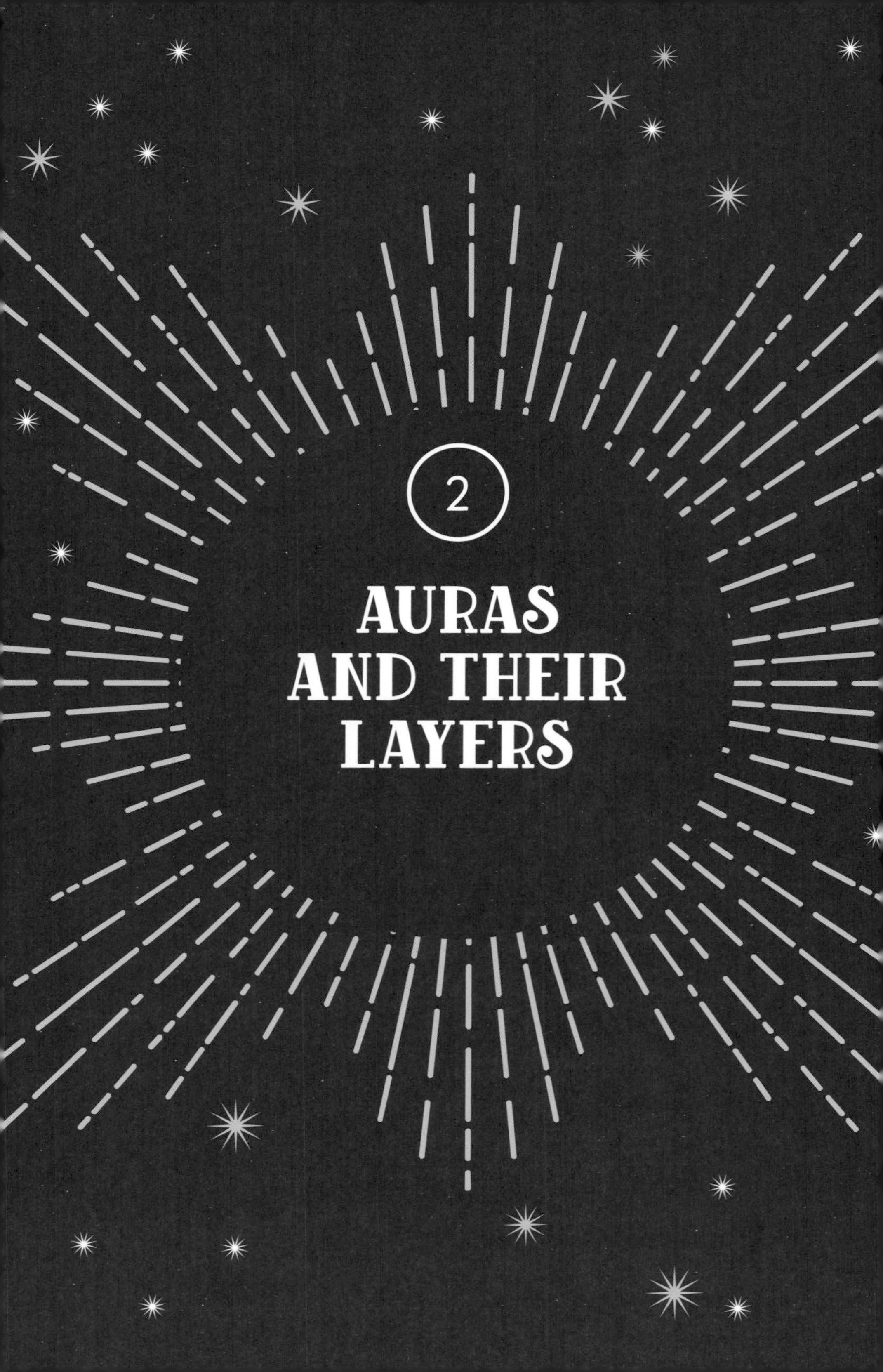

2

AURAS AND THEIR LAYERS

Our auras reflect our physical, mental, emotional, and spiritual well-being, and understanding this connection can help us respond to life with awareness rather than just reacting to situations. We now know science is beginning to prove what esoteric teachers around the world have said throughout the ages.

The first step to creating this awareness is understanding the body's three-fold energy system that consists of our aura, our chakras, and our meridian system. Physical, emotional, mental, spiritual, and past-life traumas are stored in the different layers of the aura and the chakras, and by healing and clearing them, you can help yourself move forward in your life. In this chapter we will explore the aura; then later we will find out about the meridian system and the chakras and how they all fit together.

Auras

We are all made up of the physical, emotional, mental, and spiritual bodies, and our aura is made up of the etheric, lower astral, higher astral, and spiritual bodies.

The etheric body is the densest energetic body. It is close to and interlinked with the physical body, and it includes all our physical senses. It has been called the etheric double, as it provides the template for the structures of the physical body. (Ether is the state between energy and matter.) It is the etheric body that we can see in Kirlian photography.

The lower astral body is less dense, and it incorporates the personality body, which is made up of ego, emotions, and our consciousness. Our thought patterns and belief structures are learned though our society and the conditioning of this physical world.

The higher astral body incorporates our unconditional emotions, such as unconditional love, acceptance, joy, as well as our mental body, which incorporates all our knowledge, learning, beliefs, rationality, and thinking patterns.

Our spiritual body holds the patterns and knowledge of our soul's experience through past lives and the soul's plan for this lifetime.

These four bodies are broken down into what are known as the seven layers of the aura.

The Seven Layers

- Etheric layer governing physical sensations
- Emotional layer governing personal feelings
- Mental layer governing our thought patterns
- Astral layer governing unconditional emotions (a bridge between physical and spiritual layers)
- Spiritual layer, which governs our ethic template and our higher will
- Celestial layer, which governs our emotional template and our higher feelings
- Causal layer connecting to our spiritual path and universal energy

Aura Layer 1
THE PHYSICAL AND ETHERIC BODIES

This is the densest of the subtle energy (also known as *prana chi*, or source energy) fields and is our electromagnetic body. It exists within us, is around every cell, and stores our vitality. It stretches 3 to 5 inches (8 to 13 cm) around the physical body and is associated with the base and sacral chakras.

Aura Layer 2
THE EMOTIONAL BODY

The emotional layer is part of both the etheric layer and the lower astral layer and is connected to our personal feelings and the sacral and solar plexus chakras. It extends 6 to 9 inches (15 to 23 cm) from the body. It's associated with feelings about the self and those desires that would master us if we didn't control them. All the chakras except the crown and root open onto this level, which carries our karma and our past-life memories. It's most commonly associated with the solar plexus chakra.

Aura Layer 3
THE MENTAL BODY

This is part of the lower astral layer and lies about 9 to 12 inches (23 to 30 cm) from the body. It's concerned with our rational and mental activity, which is constantly changing. Negative thought forms attract negativity while positive thought forms attract positive influences in our lives. This layer holds all we have learned in our lifetime. Our thoughts have a direct relationship to how we feel, so this layer is associated with both the solar plexus chakra and the throat chakra.

Aura Layer 4
THE ASTRAL BODY

This layer extends 12 inches (30 cm) or more away from the body and connects to the heart chakra. It's associated with love and acts as a bridge between the lower chakras, connecting us to this physical life and the higher chakras of our spiritual being. This is where all intuitive activity takes place. A great deal of subconscious interaction also takes place on this level, where there is no division between the soul and the personality.

Aura Layer 5
THE SPIRITUAL BODY

This layer extends about 2 to 3 feet (60 to 90 cm) from the physical body, and it relates to the interaction of the personality, the soul, and divine will. This level is associated with learning to trust, so it's the level we tune into when we like someone or dislike them, or when we feel that something is wrong. Our personality is the combination of all our life patterns, both those learned from experience and those inherited from our DNA and culture. This level reflects our everyday emotional and mental state. It is connected to the brow and sacral chakras as well as the throat chakra.

Aura Layer 6
THE CELESTIAL BODY

This level is more subtle than the others, and it relates to our finer feelings and our divine qualities, such as unconditional love, compassion, courage, and higher aspirations. It's the plane of meditation rather than thought and of contemplation rather than analysis. It extends much farther from the body, so it can reach out as far as 5 feet (1.5 m). It's the level at which we connect with energies from other dimensions, such as those who have died and our spirit guides. It's the level of inspiration and the template for feelings about the self. The soul is nourished at this level by the beauty of nature, music, art, meditation, and prayer. We need to appreciate others, honor, and respect them, and feel grateful to them if we are to attain this level of consciousness. It connects to the brow and crown chakras.

Aura Layer 7

CAUSAL BODY

This is the layer that connects to the crown chakra and to universal energy. At this layer we can experience spiritual ecstasy and times when we feel our connection with the universe. This layer can extend far and wide, and when our consciousness reaches this level, we are at one with the creator. It's the strongest and most resilient layer, containing the main current that runs up and down the spine, nourishing the whole body. This is the layer of pure creative thought. At this level of consciousness, we understand the perfect pattern of things (as above so below) and become enlightened. This layer also contains the astral data bank for this lifetime, which is commonly known as the soul's purpose or life's purpose. It's connected to the crown chakra but also the base chakra.

3

AURAS RELATING TO CHAKRAS

The seven layers of the aura interact with all our chakras, of which it is said that there are more than 189 in the physical body and more than 72,000 in the seven layers of the aura, but we will only be focusing on the seven major chakras in this book.

The word *chakra* in Sanskrit means "wheel." Chakras are spinning energy vortices, which are funnel-shaped with the wider, spinning end interacting with the auric field, while the stem is embedded in the spine. The vortices flow from the middle of the body, out through the front and back.

The seven major chakras run down the center of the body, roughly aligning with the spine, and they interconnect with all seven levels of the aura, operating in both the etheric and astral fields. They are each associated with a different color, and they interact with the aura, influencing its colors. The chakras each govern specific parts of the body, and they develop at different ages and store much information about our physical, emotional, mental, and spiritual health. If our chakras are balanced and functioning efficiently, we are happy and healthy and our auras are bright. If they are not, then we feel dull, fatigued, lethargic, frustrated, depressed, angry, and so on, and our auras will reflect this. By being able to see, sense, and feel chakras and auras, we can use tools and techniques (which are covered later in this book) to rebalance ourselves and regain our health.

The Energy System

Chakras act like step-down transformers that convert subtle energy that is used by the hormonal, nervous, and cellular systems of our physical bodies. We fuel our physical bodies with air, food, and water but the chakras also take in the subtle energy surrounding us, which is also fundamental for our well-being.

Rather like blood vessels carrying life-giving blood to all areas of the body, this subtle energy is carried by the meridian system that connects the chakras within our physical bodies to our auras and the energy fields surrounding us all.

This probably sounds complicated, but to put it simply, think about a local road network, and imagine the meridians as roads and the chakras as circles and intersections. The energy comes in, moves around, and flows out. With roads, traffic circles and intersections can be small or large depending upon the amount of traffic, and the same is true with the meridian system. Sometimes the energy flows freely but at other times it can get stuck, as traffic does after an accident or during road work.

If we get into an accident, even just a simple cut, we give it attention by cleaning it and putting a bandage on, and in time it heals. A bad cut usually leaves a scar on the physical body. If it is a serious accident, our bodies may carry physical scars but they will also carry emotional and mental scars, which don't always quite heal.

The traumas that we suffer during our lives are basically like traffic accidents. The traumas get stuck in our bodies and are reflected in our energy system causing the same type of blockage as a car crash or road work. If there are blockages anywhere in our energy system, in either the chakras, meridians, or aura, the energy is not flowing freely and we become, tired, lethargic, and ill. A blockage within the energy system can show where a future health issue may be developing.

Each of these major energy centers is concerned with a certain area of life, relating to physical, emotional, mental, and spiritual states. Each one governs an aspect of the physical body in association with our endocrine glands, and each governs the etheric body via the nervous system. Each one develops at different times, while for some people the higher ones never develop at all. Knowing how each chakra functions gives a greater understanding of a person's physical, psychological, and spiritual state, which is useful when giving someone healing.

As a person develops spiritually and begins to identify, heal, and release past traumas and negative patterns, their chakras and auras will vibrate at a higher level, and this can be sensed in their auras. The spin patterns of the chakras will change, and the colors will change, but more on this later.

The Base Chakra

Sanskrit Name: *Muladhara*
Auric Correspondences: Layers 1 and 7, the etheric and the causal bodies
Color: Red
Location: The base of the spine just below the pubic bone. It has the densest vibration and the slowest rate of rotation.
Sense: Smell
Deals With: This chakra governs our survival on the physical plane, so it connects us to the planet and governs not only our evolutionary cycle but also the fight-flight-freeze response.
Age: It's the first to develop, so it rules us from birth to about two to three years of age. This is when children think the whole world revolves around them before becoming aware of separateness.
Glands: This chakra governs the adrenal glands that are located above the kidneys and govern the fight-flight-freeze response for survival in the physical world. This is the only chakra where an endocrine gland is not directly over the chakra's physical zone.
Task: The base chakra is linked to the elimination of solid waste. It stands as a metaphor for getting rid of things that are no longer useful, so it rules "letting go." It governs the kidneys, colon, spinal column, legs, and bones.

Sacral Chakra

Sanskrit Name: *Svadhisthana*
Auric Correspondences: Layers 1, 2, and 5, the etheric, emotional, and spiritual bodies
Color: Orange
Location: Just above the pubic bone to just below the navel
Sense: Taste
Deals With: Everything to do with our relationships
Age: It develops between the ages of three and five but can continue to develop until the age of eight, as we discover separateness and learn to fit in with our family and the wider world.
Glands and Organs: All reproductive organs—ovaries, testicles, prostate, genitals, womb
Task: The survival of the species through reproduction. It defines our biological being and influences our social functions and activities, including the way we relate to ourselves and the way others relate to us, along with romantic relationships.

Solar Plexus Chakra

Sanskrit Name: *Manipura*
Auric Correspondences: Layers 2 and 3, the emotional and mental bodies
Color: Yellow
Location: Just above the navel to just below the diaphragm
Sense: Sight

Deals With: It governs emotions, creativity, and decision-making.
Age: It develops between the ages of five and eight and a half years old, approximately when we become aware of the wider world and how we fit into it.
Glands and Organs: Digestive system, pancreas, adrenals, stomach, liver, gallbladder, nervous system, muscles
Tasks: The digestive system is responsible for breaking down food and converting it into energy. Its physical function governs the emotional plane and the ability to sense people's physical and emotional feelings. In psychic terms, this is known as *clairsentience.* The metaphor of digestion relates to the way energy is utilized by the body and how energy is used for the soul's purpose.

Heart Chakra

Sanskrit Name: *Anahata*
Auric Correspondence: Layer 4, the astral body
Color: Green of the physical heart and sometimes pink of the higher heart
Location: Center of the body, under the breastbone by the heart
Sense: Touch

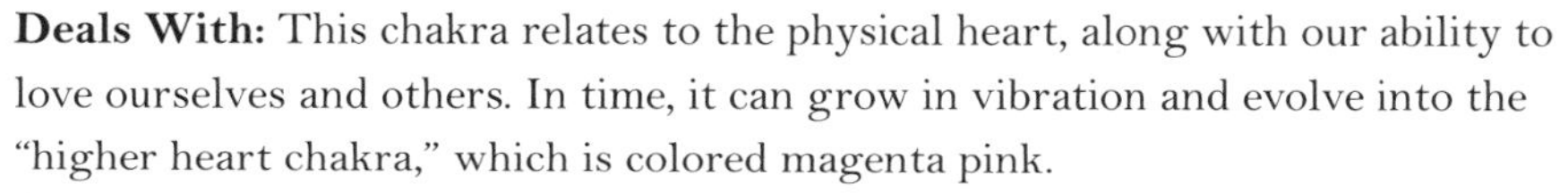

Deals With: This chakra relates to the physical heart, along with our ability to love ourselves and others. In time, it can grow in vibration and evolve into the "higher heart chakra," which is colored magenta pink.
Age: It develops between the ages of twelve to sixteen, as we learn about loving others.
Glands and Organs: Thymus gland, heart, circulatory system, arms, hands, lungs
Tasks: The ability to feel and demonstrate unconditional love and compassion for all. It connects the lower chakras with the higher chakras, and the physical with the spiritual body. It governs our empathy for others, our relationship with ourselves, and our sense of purpose. Our arms and hands reach out to others, and our lungs take in oxygen. Our heart pumps blood to all areas of the body, so it is our life force. It connects to the fourth astral layer of unconditional emotions, as it is the bridge between physical and spiritual layers.

Throat Chakra

Sanskrit Name: *Vishuddha*
Auric Correspondences: Layers 3 and 5, the mental and spiritual bodies
Color: Turquoise blue
Location: In the throat
Sense: Hearing
Deals With: Self-expression, trust, freedom. As we develop these qualities and freely express ourselves, the chakra becomes more turquoise.
Age: It develops between the ages of fifteen and twenty-one, as we are learning to express ourselves.
Glands and Organs: Thyroid, parathyroid, hypothalamus, throat, mouth, neck, arms

Tasks: Governs our thought processes, self-expression, speech, and conceptual creativity and activity. From a psychic perspective, it governs *clairaudience,* which is the ability to hear spirit voices or to speak their words in trance.

Brow Chakra

Sanskrit Name: *Ajna*
Auric Correspondences: Layers 5 and 6, the spiritual and celestial bodies
Color: Indigo
Location: Middle forehead, between the eyes
Sense: Also known as the third-eye chakra, it does not govern any particular sense but enables all the senses to work together at a deeper level and via inner vision to enable people to become intuitive.
Deals With: Inner vision, imagination, and image-making
Age: It develops from age twenty-one and on, but it never develops at all in some people.
Glands and Organs: Pituitary gland, left eye, nose, ears
Tasks: The mental plane, developing what is known psychically as *clairvoyance,* because it links with the ability to see images, patterns, colors, and symbols clearly in the mind's eye.

Crown Chakra

Sanskrit Name: *Sahasrara*
Auric Correspondences: Layers 6 and 7, the celestial and causal bodies
Color: Violet (although it can be white because all the colors of the rainbow merge in it)
Location: Top of the head, at the fontanels in the middle of the brain
Sense: None of the five traditional senses, but it allows us to connect to our soul selves and to other divine beings such as angels.
Deals With: Connects and manages right- and left-brain functions
Age: Adulthood or never
Glands and Organs: Pineal gland, cerebral cortex, central nervous system, right eye
Tasks: Governs our ability to perceive truth without facts or reasoning. It's believed the soul leaves the body through the crown chakra after death,

although some cultures believe it leaves through the heart and others believe it's through the throat. Its function is to connect us to our spiritual selves and the spiritual plane. This chakra is open in a young child, which is why they can see things we don't. It usually closes as we grow up, but it can open again as adults when we clear our lower chakras of childhood issues and traumas and raise our vibrations to the spiritual realms.

How the Layers of the Aura and Chakras Interact

We naturally assume it's our bodies that create the energy field of the aura, but it is the other way around, because we are, after all, spiritual beings that happen to be having a human physical life. The healthier we are physically, the more universal energy flows effortlessly through us, creating harmony and balance in our bodies and our lives. This energy connects to each of us through the base chakra. Our auras and our chakras are linked, and they share information by passing the energy back and forth between them. The energy in our auras reflects the energy in our chakras, but the aura also reflects the influences of

other energies around us, such as sunshine, birds, or water. Other people also influence our energy, and that is reflected back to us through our auras.

When we are happy and healthy with no issues or problems, we have fully functioning, clean chakras with bright and shiny auras. At that time, we are living happy and harmonious lives in line with our soul's purpose. Unfortunately, this does not describe most of us, and any imbalances within our physical, emotional, mental, or spiritual bodies are reflected in our chakras and in our auras. Therefore, being able to see, sense, or feel auras enables us to discover what and where any issues may be focused and to take steps to remedy and heal ourselves and others.

The good news is there are some very simple tools and techniques we can use to unblock and balance our chakras and cleanse our auras, which can bring about a happy and rewarding life. We will look at these later, but in the meantime, we need to develop our senses so we can see, sense, and feel auras.

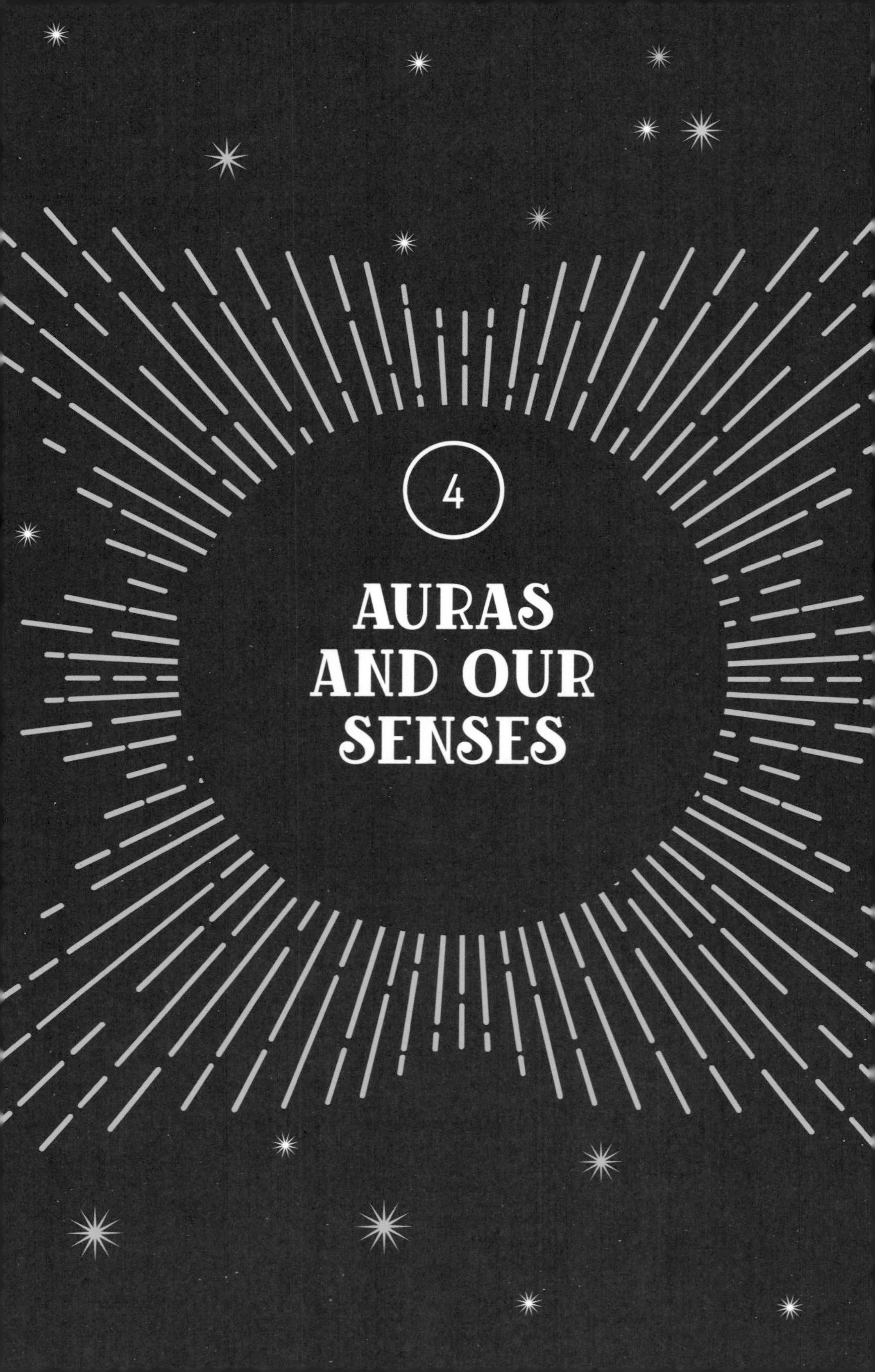

4

AURAS AND OUR SENSES

Living beings automatically sense the auras of others, and animals are particularly sensitive to auras. Dogs just seem to know when something is right or wrong. We also sometimes "just know," but unlike dogs we don't necessarily trust our inner knowing. We often take instant likes and dislikes to people or places, but we don't know why. We often feel that someone is not well or unhappy, even though they are not showing any signs of illness or depression. Obviously, some people are more sensitive to these states than others, but most of us are sensitive to feelings and needs to some degree. So how and why do we sense these things?

The Sixth Sense

What happens is that our own aura comes up against another person's aura and we start to sense what is happening. We do this automatically and completely unconsciously, and that's what generates the feeling that we like or dislike the person. It leads us to ask if everything is okay or want to run away because we don't want to be involved. We "just know." But what is this inner knowing?

It has many names, such as gut feeling, sixth sense, intuition, and even psychic ability. They are all correct. These feelings are the combination of our five traditionally recognized senses: seeing, hearing, feeling, tasting, and smelling. The only difference is the degree to which we focus on them and trust them.

Most of us trust what we see and what we experience. If we found a burn on our hand, we would know that we had touched something hot, although the same is true if we touch something very cold—if something is cold enough, it can also burn us. So, if we have a burn, did it come from something hot or cold? We know the answer because we have combined our feeling of pain with what we have seen—perhaps a red-hot poker—that we touched. We may even have smelled burning flesh, so we know it was hot. If it had been cold, we would probably have seen ice stuck to our fingers, and then we would have known our burn came from cold.

Therefore, by developing each of our senses individually, we develop the ability to see and sense auras. From birth, each one of us has developed and used our senses to survive in our world. We learn what the unconscious signs are that say, "Yes, mommy is in a good mood, and I can ask for something," or, "No, this is the time to stay away and leave her alone."

Everyone has a predominant sense—the sense that is sharpest for them—but all the senses can be enhanced with practice. Like a muscle in the body, the more you use and trust a sense, or a combination of senses, the more it will develop, and this is what psychics and empaths do; they practice and develop their senses. In fact, many of us have needed to develop acute sensitivity to survive a difficult childhood!

Your Predominant Sense

First, let's discover which is your predominant sense. Once you have that figured out, we will go on to specific exercises that will develop all of your senses.

Write down your answers to the following questions:

- What did you have for breakfast?
- What was your favorite holiday?
- What part of the world would you like to visit?
- What will your next home be like?
- How did you receive the answers to the questions? Did the answers come as pictures, thoughts, feelings, smells, a voice in your mind?

Now look to see what type of words you wrote to describe your answers. Are they seeing words, hearing words, feeling words, or thinking words?

- If you received images in your mind and wrote *seeing* words, then your predominant sense is your eyes and seeing.
- If you heard a voice in your mind and used *hearing* words, then your predominant sense is hearing.
- If you sensed and felt things and used emotional words, then your predominant sense is *feeling*.
- If you thought things and wrote *thinking* words, your predominant sense is your mind. Though thinking is not part of the traditional five sense, it is an important way in which we experience and understand the world, so we will consider it a sense of our purposes.

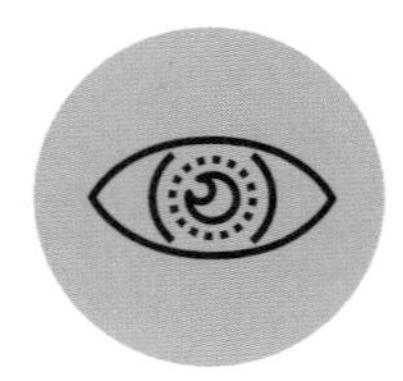

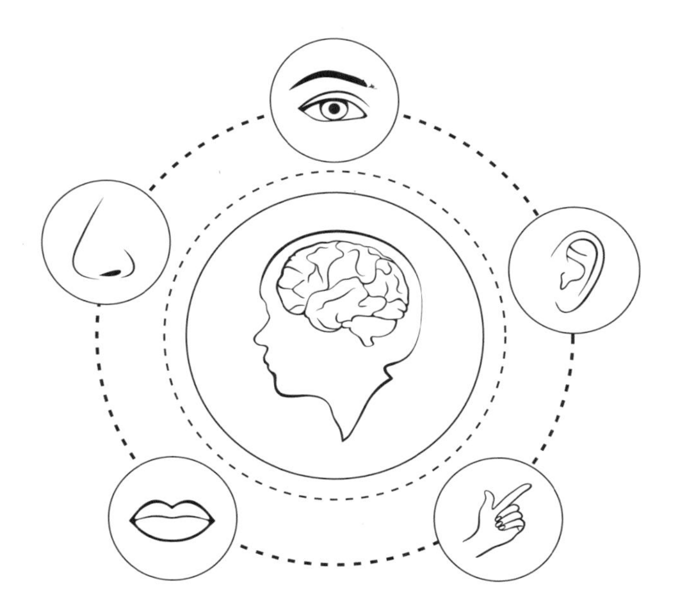

Smell and taste are also main senses, but they are not usually as dominant as seeing, hearing, feeling, and thinking, but practicing smelling and tasting different foods will enhance these senses as well as help you enjoy your meals more. In fact, smell and taste can be extremely strong anchors to memories and situations in your past.

Tip

Your childhood experiences will influence your current likes and dislikes of various smells, and if you dislike a smell, you might feel uncomfortable and tense when you encounter it.

Of course, you can have more than one sense that is strong, and you probably already unconsciously combine two or three. Most of us do this, but by practicing various exercises, you will learn to use each of them individually and also together. Most people want to be clairvoyant and "see" things—because it is the easiest psychic ability to understand—but discovering your predominant sense is more important. By practicing exercises for each sense, you will discover how they work together, and you will be able to see, sense, and feel your own aura and those of others.

Developing Your Senses

Developing all your senses is an important part of working with the aura, and the more you practice, the better and more accurate your senses will become. The more you fine-tune your senses, the more you will sense auras and the information they hold. One of the things that's most important when developing any of your senses is to ensure you're totally relaxed and focused. A quick way of relaxing is to focus on your breathing for a few moments, which really is the beginning of meditation. By focusing on your breathing, you bring your attention to yourself and to your senses.

Most everyone has the senses of seeing, hearing, feeling, tasting, smelling, and, for our purposes, we will include thinking as well. You have already discovered your primary sense, but the primary sense is not the same for everyone. We all take in millions of pieces of information every second of the day. Some people's brains give priority to what they see, others are more in tune with what they hear, while some are more into what they feel or think. Regardless which sense is naturally your strongest, it is by honing and combining all the senses that we develop our sixth sense, which enables us to see, sense, and feel auras and to be able to work with them for ourselves and others in order to bring our lives in line with our soul's purpose so we can live richly rewarding happy lives.

Another important aspect of sensing and working with the aura is using your imagination. If you're waiting for something to happen, then that's all that is going on: you're waiting and nothing is happening. If you start to imagine things, then you can usually see and sense a lot more. For instance, if you can't "see" the color of an aura, what color would you imagine it to be? Whatever you image helps your ability to sense to get past the logical left brain. The imagining helps make the reality.

Practicing all the exercises below will enable you to develop each sense individually while you also learn how you process information. You will refine your predominant sense as well as all the other senses, thus making it easier for your unconscious senses to pass information to your conscious mind and thus improve your ability to see, sense, feel, smell, and touch auras.

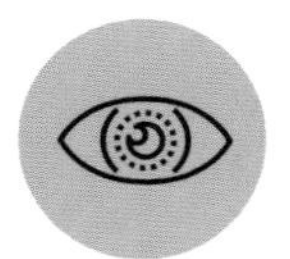

Exercises for Developing Your Visual Sense

EXERCISE 1
IMAGINE YOUR AURA

- Imagine you are looking at yourself in a mirror.
- Imagine your aura surrounding you, and look at all of it.
- What do you imagine is the overall color?
- Then look to the left and the right.
- Is what you are seeing similar or different?
- If different, how different?
- Then look at the top and the bottom. How different are they?
- How many different colors are there, and how dense are they?

You can also do this exercise by visualizing each of your chakras and watching to see how they spin—freely or sluggishly—and whether there are any dark shapes in them. This is a very useful exercise that can be used for self-healing through the aura and chakras.

EXERCISE 2
SELF EXAMINATION

Sit in a comfortable position and focus on your breathing to bring yourself into a meditative state. With your eyes closed, "look" at the inside of your body, part by part, organ by organ, imaging what they each look like from the inside. Perhaps have an imaginary conversation with your chakras and your aura to see if there is anything they need. Sometimes a chakra might want a certain color to boost its energy. On another occasion it might want to be loved more. You and your chakras are only limited by what you imagine.

EXERCISE 3
CLOUD GAZING

Look up at the sky and watch the clouds. What shapes do you see?

EXERCISE 4
WHO'S CALLING?

When the phone rings, before you answer it (or look at it the caller ID), close your eyes and imagine who is on the other end. You can do this before the phone even rings by imagining who will be the next person to call you.

Notice how this information comes to you. Do you see a picture of the person in your mind? Do you hear their voice, or do you think of them? It doesn't matter which, but the answer will give you an indication of your primary sense.

EXERCISE 5
AUTOSTEREOGRAMS

Search on the internet for *autostereograms*—those images of dots that create 3-D pictures—print them out, soften your gaze, and see what pictures you can see.

Exercises for Developing Your Auditory Sense

For these exercises, you will need to close your eyes.

EXERCISE 1
OUTSIDE

Go outside and listen. What can you hear? First notice the sounds closest to you, then focus your attention and become aware of sounds farther in the distance. What are they? Are they birds, rain, wind, trees, traffic, planes 3 miles (5 km) up?

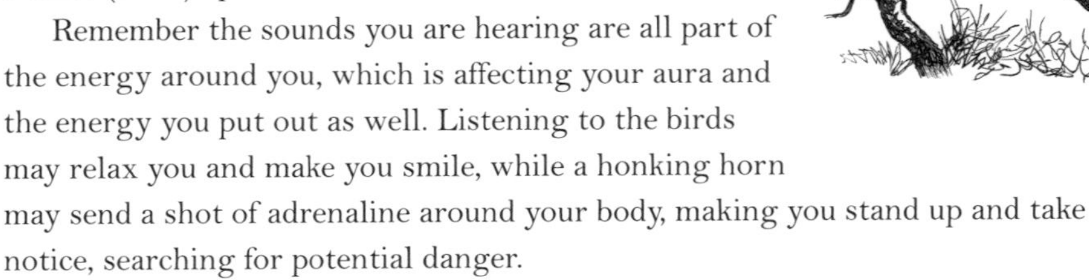

Remember the sounds you are hearing are all part of the energy around you, which is affecting your aura and the energy you put out as well. Listening to the birds may relax you and make you smile, while a honking horn may send a shot of adrenaline around your body, making you stand up and take notice, searching for potential danger.

The energies around us reflected in sound reverberate within our auras. Even sounds that are above or below our normal hearing levels will be absorbed and processed by our auras.

EXERCISE 2
OTHER PEOPLE'S SENSES

The next time you talk to someone, listen to how they are talking to you. Can you identify their predominant sense? What type of words are they using? Are they using seeing, hearing, or feeling words? Try this with a few people.

This is a very useful exercise if you choose to give aura readings to people, because you can ensure they understand what you're saying by using their way of communicating rather than yours. This makes it much easier for them to understand and accept what you are saying to them. It's also extremely useful in preventing misunderstandings in relationships with family, friends, colleagues, and that all-important romantic one.

EXERCISE 3
LISTEN TO YOUR SELF

- Sit comfortably and focus on the inside of your body.
- Listen to what you can hear. For instance, is your stomach rumbling? If it is, is it saying you are hungry or have gas?
- Can you hear your heartbeat? Is it regular or erratic, and what does that tell you?
- Is there a ringing in your ears?
- Can you hear a high-pitch hum? Many people who naturally use their hearing more will occasionally hear a high-pitch hum. This is the hum above the normal human hearing range, and the vibrations come from the higher dimensions. If you can't hear it now, don't worry; it will develop with time and practice.

This exercise helps you take the time to notice your own inner workings, and if you practice it often, you will notice more and more, allowing you to gather more information from both your own aura and the auras of others.

Exercises for Developing Your Feelings

As we learned earlier, the combination of our five senses makes our so-called sixth sense, which is nothing more than our five senses being well developed and working together. We can use this sixth sense to detect auras after we have taken the time and trouble to hone the five senses and learn how they communicate with us. At the end of the day, the information gleaned by all our senses is processed in microseconds by our brains, and it comes together as a "feeling." Some of which we understand and some we don't. We "just know," but we don't necessarily know how we know. At this point, these feelings are usually called intuition and sometimes psychic ability.

EXERCISE 1
FEEL YOUR SELF

Sit comfortably and focus on the inside of your body. What can you feel? Start at the top of your head and work down to your toes. If it helps, touch the part of the body you're sensing and notice how it feels. What sensations are you experiencing both in your body and in your hands?

EXERCISE 2
ILLUMINATION

Imagine white light coming down through your crown and passing through your body. Notice how it feels. Is it flowing freely, or are there parts of the body where it seems to get stuck? If so, notice and perhaps ask what is causing it or what it needs to get it moving again.

Remember that any blockages you sense in the physical body will be reflected in your aura. Later we will be doing exercises within the aura to remove those blockages both within the aura and within the body.

EXERCISE 3
CRYSTAL WORK

- Take a crystal (see pages 112–117 for more information about using crystals with auras) and hold it in your hand. Close your eyes and notice what you feel. Is it cold? Warm? Does it have a vibration? If so, how does the vibration feel? Is it just in your hand or is it passing up through your wrist and the rest of your arm?
- Try it with a different crystal. What do you feel with this one? How different is it?

Make some notes, and after you have practiced with a few crystals, try different crystals in each hand. The purpose of this exercise is for you to begin to notice the different vibrations of energy. Everything in the world vibrates. Science tells us that nothing in the world is solid; matter is just trillions of atoms vibrating at different frequencies, which is reflected as different densities. Everything is energy, whether we can see, sense, or feel it. We can't see hot or cold, but we still know whether something is hot or cold because of what we feel and due to our past experiences. Physically we can't see light, but we know it is light because if it is dark, we can't see anything. As you experience things in their physical form, such as feeling a crystal, you will recognize and notice those same vibrations again when you start to feel auras that seem to tell you something.

EXERCISE 4
COLOR WORK

Every color holds its own vibration, and being able to sense colors in an aura is very important—especially if your primary mode of processing information is sensing. (But keep in mind that not everyone is clairvoyant, and not everyone will be able to see things even with practice. Also, see chapter 6 for more information about using colors and auras.)

- Gather some envelopes or bags as well as some objects of different colors, such as paper or ribbons.
- Place each color object in an envelope or bag and mix them all up so you don't know which is which.
- Take one and hold it between your hands close to your body.
- Close your eyes and focus on the energy between your hands.

- What do you sense?
- How does it feel?
- What color might it be?
- Now hold the envelope or bag 6 to 12 inches (15 to 30 cm) from your body and notice what you feel in your hands. Alternatively you could put the envelope or bag on a table and hold your hands 6 to 12 inches (15 to 30 cm) above it and see what your hands sense.
- Does it hold a similar vibration to any of the colors you have been experiencing?
- If so, this is probably the color of that part of your aura, which at that distance will likely be either the second layer (the emotional body) or third layer (mental body) of your aura.

EXERCISE 5
MINDFUL MEALS

You can also develop your senses of taste and smell. As you're preparing a meal, notice what each vegetable feels like, what it smells like, and once cooked, focus on the flavor of each individual mouthful. Notice how it feels in your mouth, what it tastes like, and how it changes as you chew. Try this with lots of different types of food and drink. Not only will you discover what you like most, you will appreciate food more. You will probably chew more thoroughly and derive more from each meal, thus improving your health and diet at the same time.

Also take notice of any memories that come to you with each smell or taste. These will help you identify areas of potential past traumas that may be causing potential illnesses or imbalances within your aura and your body.

The purpose of this exercise is to hone your senses of smell and taste because when sensing someone's aura, you may well sense a particular smell or taste, which in itself may be nothing, but which, on the other hand, may tell you a great deal. This is especially so if there is a metallic taste, which means that the person whose aura you are sensing needs added minerals for health, or it could show that the person has a hip or knee replacement. A coppery taste at the scene of an accident could be an indication of internal bleeding.

For information on healing the aura through food, see page 127.

Exercises for Developing Your Thinking

Clear thinking (claircognizance) influences all your feelings and is part of your inner "knowing." Everything you think about affects the way you feel, and it affects the energy that is reflected in your aura. For many people, intuition comes as thoughts or flashes of insight which can appear to come from nowhere but are in fact unconscious ideas that are becoming conscious. What we unconsciously sense about an aura will become a thought that enters the right-hand creative side of the brain. You "know" without knowing how you know. Memories, on the other hand, come to us from the left side of the brain. Practicing thinking and controlling your thoughts will help you develop the imagination and trust you need in your own thoughts that will allow you to sense and work with auras.

EXERCISE 1
WORRY

Most of us worry about things at some time or another, but what does worrying actually achieve for us other than lowering our energy and dulling our auras? In fact, if you think about it, worrying is just our imaginations focusing on all the things that could go wrong. Fortunately, we can turn this negative energy into something positive.

- Think about something that's been worrying you lately.
- List all the things that can go "wrong."
- What would be the worst outcome?
- What are the odds on that happening?
- Make a few contingency plans for that outcome if you wish.
- Now start to think about how it can go "right."
- What is the best possible outcome?
- What are the chances of that happening?
- What actions can you take to assist in creating the most likely positive outcome?

If you get stuck, then think about what you would say to a friend who had this problem. Notice how you change your whole reality in the space of a moment.

EXERCISE 2
STRESS AND ANXIETY

When you are stressed, worried, or anxious about something, take a moment to think about what you are grateful for in your life. It may be something as simple such as the sunshine, or the fact you have a roof over your head, unlike so many in the world. Or better still, you can consider your good qualities, your compassion and your empathy, your ability to read and learn and experience new things. Or perhaps something good you would like to have in your life. It could be a big thing like a long vacation or a new job, or it could be a small thing like an ice cream sundae. Just focus on thinking about it for a few minutes. What would it be like to give yourself this gift? After all you deserve it.

EXERCISE 3
IMAGINATION

Developing your imagination is crucial to aura work, and this exercise will really help you develop your mental creative skills.

- Think about what it would be like to be a bovine animal, what its life might be like.
- What type of creature would you be? A bull, a dairy cow, or maybe a calf?
- Think about how these animals live.
- Do you think they are happy being bovine or do you think they would prefer to be a horse or a goat?
- Do you think each animal gets along better with some members of its herd than others?
- Do they worry about tomorrow?
- What would they say to you if they could talk?

Write a few notes about what you have learnt about being a cow and how that new knowledge can be incorporated into your life.

EXERCISE 4
THOUGHTFUL MEDITATION

- Make yourself comfortable and focus on your breathing.
- Just notice the temperature of the air coming in through your nose and the temperature going out through your mouth.

- Breathing naturally, just notice whether you are breathing from your chest or your abdomen.
- Spend some time focusing on your breathing and just notice what thoughts pop into your mind.
- Follow your thoughts to see where they lead.
- Observe your thoughts but don't judge them, because they are not good or bad thoughts—they just are.
- If you can, notice where they come from. Do they seem to arise from your left or right side of your brain? Or do they start somewhere in your body before they rise up into your mind?
- Bring your attention back to your breath, then slowly open your eyes and come back to the outside world.

EXERCISE 5
MINDFULNESS

This exercise will help you to notice how your thoughts influence your feelings.

- Think for a few moments about a time in your life you would rather forget.
- Notice how you feel. Notice your physiology.
- Think about how you are standing or sitting. Are you slumped over or slouching?
- If so straighten up, smile, and see how that changes the way you feel.
- What thoughts come into your head now?

EXERCISE 6
LESSONS LEARNED

Think about how much you have learned about auras and energy so far. What did you hope to learn when you first picked up this book? Reflect about the exercises you have done. Notice which exercises you found easy and which ones were difficult. Think about how you are going to be able to use this knowledge and what positive outcomes there are going to be as you put these lessons into practice. Think about what more you are going to be able to do when you have finished this book. What insights have you received about yourself so far? Make some notes so you can refer back to them as you continue through the book.

❋ ❋ ❋

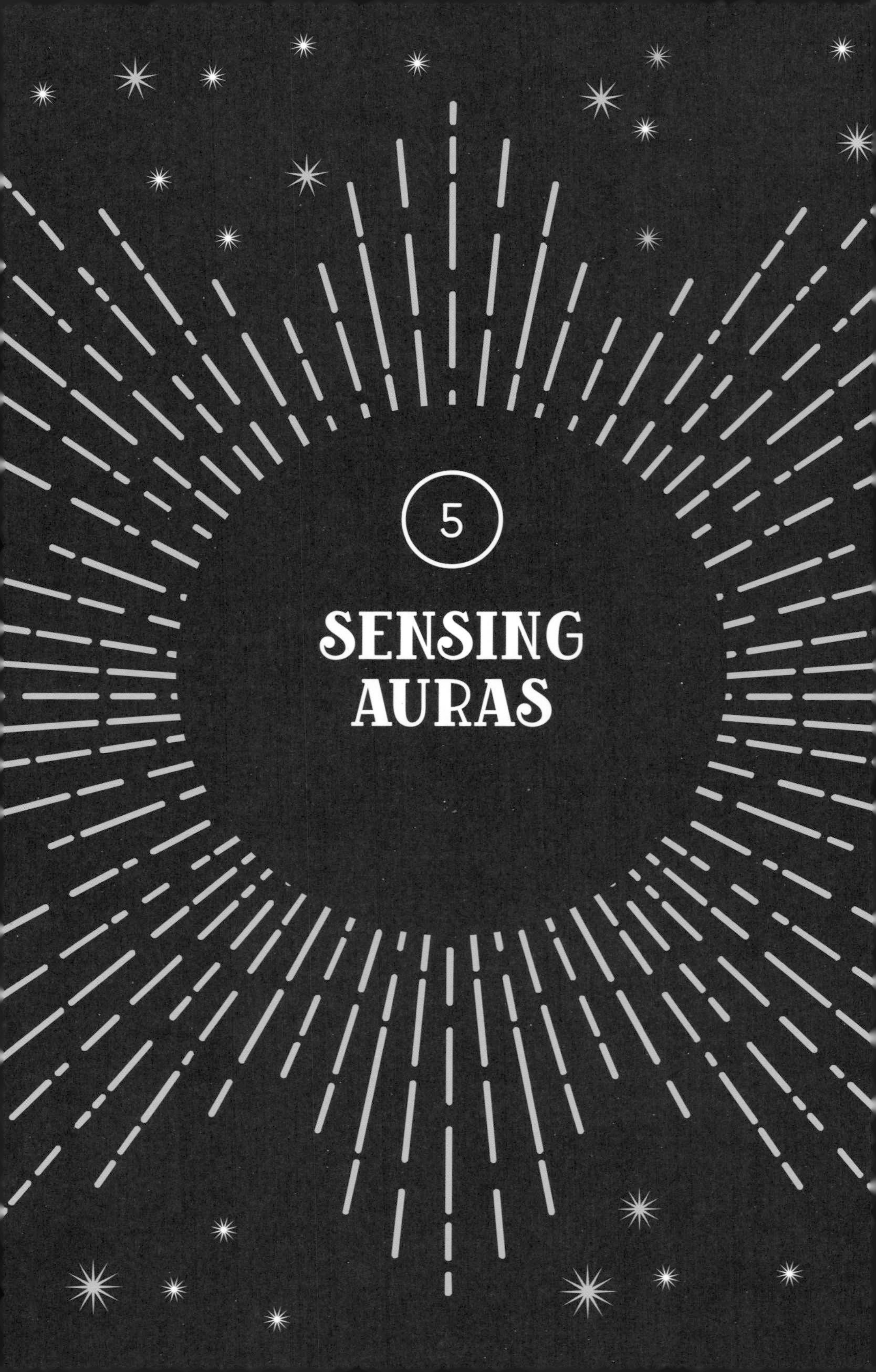

5

SENSING AURAS

The more you practice, the better you will become at seeing and sensing the energies around you, especially the auras of others. If you feel you aren't getting it right to start with don't worry, just keep going. If after a while you still feel you're not getting anywhere and that you will never be able to see or sense an aura, don't give up. It just means you need to use your imagination more. Be sure to exercise your imagination, because a lot of the time, whatever you are imagining is what you're unconsciously sensing, and exercising your imagination will help you bring your unconscious into consciousness.

The Importance of Imagination

Do not underestimate the power of your unconscious to sense things. A good example of this is when you are focusing on your phone while walking down a street and you're about to cross the road but suddenly you take a step back from the curb because your senses warn about a bus that's coming down the road, which, if you had stepped off the curb, would have hit you. The reality of this unconscious action is that you were distracted and hadn't heard the bus but when it entered your auric field, you took an instinctive step back out of harm's way.

Even with experiences like that, we often don't trust our senses and we start to rationalize. How many times have you thought you heard something and decided it was your imagination, just to find out that you *had* heard something? Or what about when you see something from the corner of your eye, but then you rationalize it away.

We live in a three-dimensional world, and as such we see and touch physical things. We are taught that if we can't see and touch something, it doesn't exist, that it's only in our imagination. But what about oxygen and carbon dioxide? We can't see them, but science tells us they are there. Well the same is true of auras, which vibrate at a higher frequency than physical bodies and so it is not easy to see them, but that doesn't mean they aren't there.

People often ask when they are learning how to be psychic how they can tell whether the information coming into their heads is from their imagination or if it is real. If it is in your imagination, it *is* real because it is the energy of the esoteric world—the etheric energy and spirit. For instance, if you imagine that there is a blockage in someone's aura, just because you're imagining it does not mean it's wrong. It just means you are learning to use your unconscious sense.

Developing and trusting your imagination is vitally important for working with auras and for sensing colors. Let's say you look at a color and imagine something that happens to be that color; for instance you imagine an orange, then the color you are sensing is orange. Or when you sense the color yellow, you might imagine a lemon. If you imagine a blue sky or sea, then those are the shades of color you are sensing. When you see or imagine a color, then those are the colors within your aura. As you open your imagination to the unseen world, it intuitively picks up on the aura and uses everyday objects to show you what your own unconscious senses are picking up.

Thought Forms

Thought forms are a combination of memory and imagination. Memories provide the foundation for new insights, new decisions, and creative acts, and help in translating what we sense into something we can understand and articulate.

When our brains are absorbing and sorting all the millions of bits of information picked up by the senses, they run the information against its databanks of stored information that comes from past experience and knowledge. A visual person will see in their mind's eye colored geometric patterns, moving pictures, or impressions that flash across the screen and that are barely perceived as pictures but almost as fleeting impressions. This is something that happens moment-by-moment to us throughout our lives. It is part of how we process information, and it is part of our psychic self.

How to See, Sense, or Feel Auras

There are many ways of seeing, sensing, and feeling auras, and the more you practice the easier it will become. I suggest you try all the following exercises to see which one comes most easily to you. To access your sixth sense, you need to be very relaxed, almost in a daydream state but still aware. If you have experience with meditation, use your chosen method to enter a meditative state. If you do not, make sure you take a few deep breaths to relax yourself and imagine you're daydreaming. Remember to use your imagination, which is so important when sensing auras and trying to heal them.

EXERCISE 1
HOW TO SEE AN AURA IN TEN MINUTES

The easiest and quickest way to learn to see auras is to do it with a friend.

- Have your friend sit comfortably in a chair with a blank wall behind them, preferably a light-colored one. If there is no light wall around, hang a white sheet behind them.
- Step back at least ten paces and settle yourself comfortably in a chair.
- Close your eyes and center yourself with three deep breaths.
- Open your eyes and stare gently past your friend's head at the gap between their shoulder and head. Soften your gaze and imagine you're looking through them to the wall behind.
- Keep staring and allow the image to become blurry and fuzzy around the edges.
- Eventually their aura will begin to appear. It may look a bit like a heat haze to start with, but with practice you will start to notice whether it's stronger on one side or the other, whether there are any colors in it, and if so, what and where they are.

Tip

If you have ever done an autostereogram (a dot picture with a 3-D form hidden in it) and found the image within the dots, then you should find this one quite easy. If you can't find a friend to help, look up 3-D pictures on the internet and practice that way.

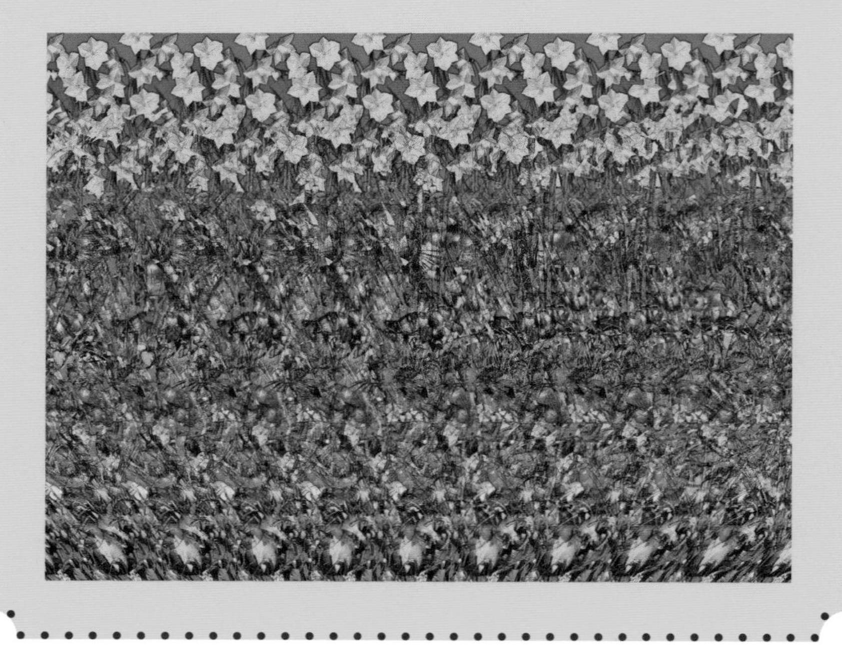

EXERCISE 2
SENSING SOMEONE'S COLOR

The next time you're ever in a lecture or a boring meeting, stare at someone in a room for a few minutes and then close your eyes. You will see the outline of the person against the back of your eyelids. What color or colors surround the image? The color you see will be the person's predominant aura color.

You can also discover your own predominant aura color by looking at yourself in a mirror and doing either of the previous two exercises. If you don't attend lectures or meetings and haven't got a willing friend or partner to practice with, pick a living thing—a pet, tree, anything against a light or dark background of a single color—and do both exercises above. If you're lucky, you will see color, but don't be disappointed if it doesn't happen. If you never see colors, you could buy an aura camera as that will definitely pick up on them.

Don't forget, practice makes perfect, and don't expect too much of yourself right away. The more you practice these two exercises, the better you will become at them.

EXERCISE 3
HOW TO FEEL YOUR AURA

Sit or stand comfortably, take a few deep breaths, and then vigorously rub your hands together. Hold your hands wide apart and slowly bring them together. As you bring them together, you will notice the energy between your hands, and your hands may tingle and bounce off the energy field. If you push through it, then the energy field will disappear.

EXERCISE 4
FEELING SOMEONE'S AURA

For this one you will need another person. Let your partner stand on one side of the room with their back to you. Go as far away from them as possible, and then, with your hands outstretched, very slowly walk toward them, letting your hands sense the energy in front of you. You will know you are in touch with the edge of your partner's aura either when your hands start to tingle or when your partner instinctively turns around.

Everyone's aura is different in size, shape, density, color, and so on, so there is no right or wrong distance with this exercise. You can ask your partner to turn around when they sense you coming into their energy field. You may need to go farther in or farther out to feel their energy for yourself. Another step you can take with this exercise is to ask your partner to imagine breathing their aura in, to within just a few inches (centimeters) of their body, and then do the exercise again, noticing how much closer you need to be before you feel anything and before they turn round.

You can also breathe your aura in on a crowded train or when you feel someone impinging on your personal space, especially if there is nowhere to move to. Just imagine you're breathing your aura in so that it's just a couple of inches (centimeters) around you. You could also imagine a good hard shell around it, protecting you from the energy of others.

You can do the same exercise as above with a plant or tree, but be aware that the energy fields of plants and trees are very different from human ones. They are a lot subtler and therefore harder to sense. The aura around a plant is usually a lot closer to the plant than with a person, while the aura of a tree can be a lot larger.

EXERCISE 5
DOWSING WITH A PENDULUM

Another way of feeling an aura is to dowse with a pendulum, which can be as simple as a weight on the end of a cord. You can make one with string and a screw or nail, or you can buy pendulums that are made of crystal or a piece of wood on a chain.

First, practice feeling the chakras within the aura. They are the strongest energy sources and therefore the easiest to sense. The differences between the energy of each chakra are also easier to distinguish than the layers of the aura, and they will tell you a lot about what is happening within the four auric bodies of a person or animal. Once you are able to sense the chakra energies, you will be able to use your pendulum or even your hands to feel the more subtle energies in the aura, and eventually you will be able to distinguish the levels.

Choose a person, plant, or animal, and hold your pendulum by the end of the string or chain so the weight is hanging. Be as steady as possible and gently move the pendulum toward your subject. When the pendulum feels the edge of the aura, it will start to vibrate, sway, or move. You can then very gently move the pendulum around and discover the size and shape of the aura of your chosen object. You could even ask your pendulum to discern different layers of the aura by holding your pendulum at the different levels and seeing how it behaves. The closer to the object, the more dramatically it will swing. The farther away in the upper astral layers it is, the more subtle the resulting energy vibration will be. Each person and each pendulum will react in different ways. By experimentation you will discover how it works for you. For some the pendulum will swing back and forth, side to side, and for others it may seem to be still with a slight vibration. You can also use this exercise on a person just by starting next to someone and then slowly moving away and seeing how your pendulum behaves.

If you are working with a person, ask them to lie down. Then hold your pendulum above the approximate position of a chakra and wait to see what it does. The easiest one to start with is the solar plexus, which is just above the navel, then try the heart or the throat. If the pendulum is swinging vigorously the chakra is functioning well, but if it's slow, then the chakra is blocked. You may find the pendulum swings in different directions on different chakras. It's quite common for chakras to spin in alternate directions, for example, clockwise for one and counterclockwise for the next.

There is no right or wrong way for the chakras to spin, they just do what they feel like, but the direction can give an indication as to where the person is on their spiritual journey. In most cases, at the start of their journey, the chakras all spin in the same direction, the lower ones being more open than the higher ones. As a person progresses, each chakra starts to spin in whatever direction it wants. Those that are open and clear will spin quickly, and those that are closed or blocked will be sluggish. These are important exercises, because using a pendulum in the aura is a very good way of cleansing and healing the aura, but more on this later.

When someone is fully open and reasonably balanced, their crown chakra will spin in a different manner, often in a flower of life pattern or as a twelve-pointed star. Both of these are rare, and in my experience the flower of life pattern is found with indigo children (see page 65) and the twelve-pointed star is found on people with autism.

Tip

Not everyone can work with a pendulum, so if your pendulum doesn't respond to chakras for you, don't worry, just use your left hand instead. The reason we use our left hand is that the left side of the body is ruled by the right, intuitive side of the brain; thus most people usually sense more in their left hand than right hand, which is better used for logical things like writing and mathematics. If you are left-handed, you must still use your left hand, because being left-handed means your intuition is probably already highly developed.

When you are confident that you can sense the chakras, then move your pendulum or your hand to detect the aura and start to dowse for the subtle changes within the four main bodies within it: the etheric, lower astral, upper astral, and spiritual levels.

Whether you're working with a pendulum or with your hands, you can practice holding your hands or pendulum at the different appropriate distances so you can notice the subtle shifts between all seven layers of the aura.

EXERCISE 6
TAKE THE TIME

The next time you meet up with a friend, sit quietly for a moment and focus on what you feel or sense about them. How do they feel to you? What is their mood? Are they happy, worried, stressed . . . ? Notice what comes into your mind, then ask them how they feel and see how accurate you are. You can do this exercise with a stranger, but it's best done with people you know because they are more likely to tell you the truth rather than just saying, "I'm fine thank you."

Other Ways of Seeing Auras

Even if you don't have much luck sensing auras with the exercises we've gone over, there is some equipment you can try that will help you to see them.

Aura Glasses

Aura glasses work by focusing cutting out ninety-five percent of the color spectrum and focusing on the UV portion of light. This intensifies the subtle energy fields, making them easier to see. Like everything else, they take a while to practice with, but they worked for me. My only reservation is that they only showed me the predominant color in the person's aura. You can easily find aura glasses for purchase online.

Aura Apps

There are apps you can download to phones and tablets that allow you to take photos of auras, but I have yet to find one that works.

Aura Cameras

Aura photography has improved by leaps and bounds since the first Kirlian cameras of the 1950s, but they all work the same way. You sit in front of a white or black cloth and place your hands on a metal plate that analyzes the electromagnetic field, which is then recorded and sent to a special camera or computer that captures the image of the energy emanating from your hands. By the 1990s, there were all sorts of different cameras on the market, and you see them being used at mind, body, spirit events. They all work the same way but focus on different aspects of the aura. Some focus on the chakras, some on the aura, and some on the energy within the body. By the 2000s, there were even cameras that took not only still photographs but also videos of how the aura constantly changes and how one aura interacts with another.

USING AN AURA CAMERA

When aura cameras were first connected to computers and started to show chakras and auras, I was personally very skeptical, despite their popularity. Computers are programmed, and therefore they are always going to show the colors that have been programmed, although this will not affect the colors within the aura captured by the camera. I tried one of these programs, and after doing a meditation to raise my vibration and to change the dimensions, the image changed immediately. The images here were taken of me with an aura camera. They show me at the start of a meditation with a normal aura. The second image is of me after the meditation, and the third is at the end of a long day's work at a psychic fair. Let's look at them in detail.

IMAGE ONE

This shows the normal state of my aura and chakras. The crown is white because when all the chakras are open, all the chakra colors are shown as white at the crown. It also shows the different colors within the aura. Lemon at the top, blue and turquoise on the sides with a touch of green, pink, and lemon at the bottom.

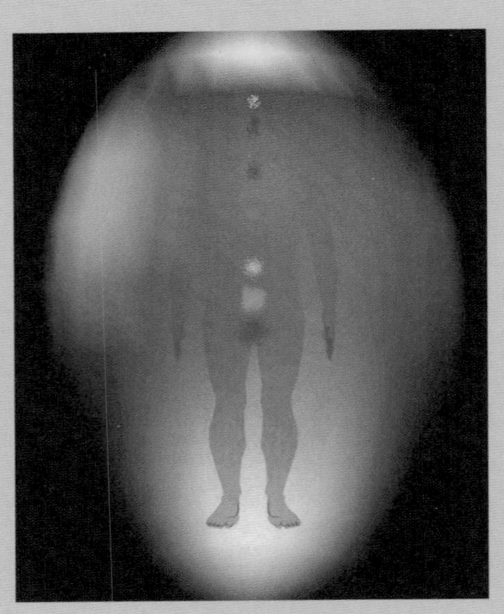

IMAGE TWO

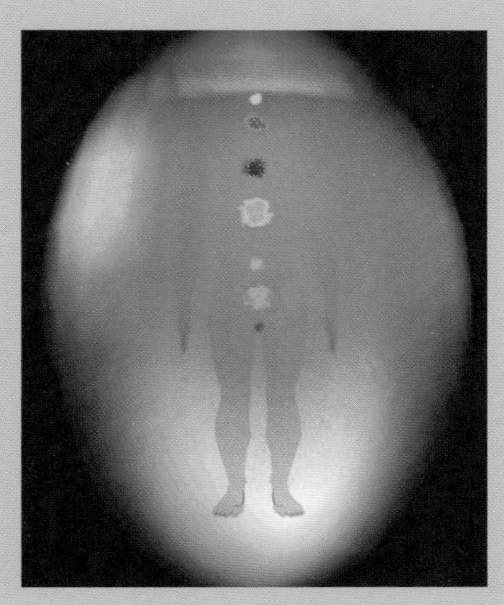

This was taken after a meditation to open to the fourth dimension. Notice the change where the heart has gone from green to pale blue with lavender in the center. Notice the magenta pink at top and bottom, flowing out into the outer layers as well as the enlarged sacral chakra throwing orange out to the edges.

IMAGE THREE

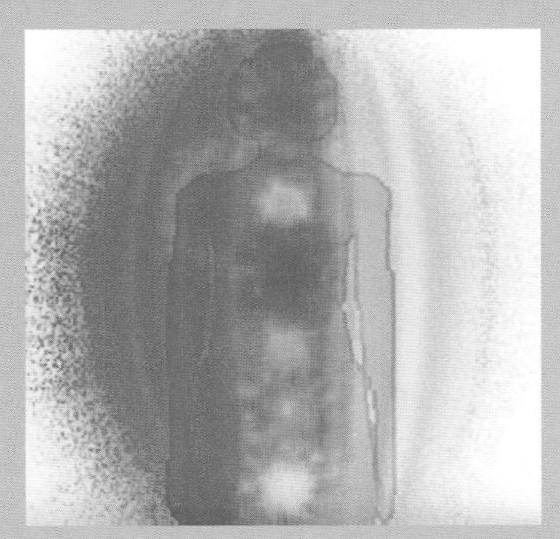

This was taken after a long day doing angel readings and bears no resemblance to anything that was programmed.

6

AURAS AND COLOR

Color is very important because each chakra has its own color, and their health and ability to function are reflected in the aura. The energy within our bodies moves through the chakras and meridian system and is then reflected in the aura, which is why we can sense the way others feel. The colors within an aura reflect what is going on within the physical, emotional, mental, and spiritual bodies of everyone and everything, either on a conscious or on an unconscious level. The aura can tell us a lot about ourselves, about others, and even about the health of plants, trees, animals, and other living creatures. The colors in the aura change from moment to moment as the aura interacts with the energies and vibrations of other auras around it, reflecting the physical, emotional, mental, and spiritual state of its owners and of other things that influence them.

Colors themselves also hold a vibration, and an aura reflects these vibrations. As we develop spiritually, our vibration changes, and those changes are reflected in our auras. Each of the colors of the rainbow vibrates at a different frequency, and some are more easily seen than others. For instance, red is the densest color, whereas violet is said to have the highest vibration. Infrared and ultraviolet aren't visible to humans, but under ultraviolet light, all sorts of unseen things are revealed. Even colors we can't see can still influence us unconsciously.

Colors are difficult to describe, and although they all vibrate at different frequencies, they are also very difficult to sense. That's why we often refer to the physical and natural world to describe colors, such as grass green, blood red, battleship gray, sky blue, sunflower yellow, and so on.

We think of color as something we see, but those who are visually impaired are able to sense colors and report that colors can feel different. For instance:

- Red feels strong and hot.
- Orange feels confident and warm.
- Yellow gets you feeling creative and focused.
- Green feels calm and can elicit the sensation of smelling trees and flowers.
- Blue brings feelings of peace.
- Indigo conjures feelings of being uplifted.
- Violet is linked to spiritual insights.

With practice, many people can become slightly clairvoyant and gain the ability to see the colors of the aura. These exercises will help you with that practice.

EXERCISE
FEEL THE COLORS

Here is a simple exercise you can do yourself to develop your sense of touch and color.

- Gather pieces of ribbon in different colors and mix them up in a box.
- With your eyes closed, pick up one ribbon and focus your energy on it. Use your sense of touch to see if you can feel anything.
- What pictures do you imagine, and what colors are they?
- If you're talking to yourself in your mind, what do you hear yourself say?
- What are you feeling—calm, hot? What sensations are passing through your body and where?
- Document your impressions by speaking into a recording device so you can listen later. Take your time—you're practicing getting in tune with your senses and how you sense information.

All this information will help you become more and more aware of how you personally interpret color. Work with two or three ribbons before you open your eyes. There is no right or wrong way to do this exercise, and there are no feelings that are right or wrong. You're just discovering how each color makes you feel, how it communicates its energy to you, and how you interpret it.

What you're doing with this exercise is starting to bring your unconscious feelings about color into consciousness as well as discovering how you interpret your unconscious assessments of people's auras when you come in contact with them in your everyday life.

Tip

When you understand how color communicates feelings to you, you'll be able to judge the auras of others by passing your hands over them. Besides those who are naturally clairvoyant, this is how most people read auras.

The Meanings of Colors

This is a big subject, and you may feel it's hard to get a handle on, but you probably already know a lot more about it than you realize. There are many sayings in our language referring to states of consciousness and color. For example:

- He's yellow, meaning cowardly.
- Seeing red, meaning being very angry.
- The green-eyed monster, meaning jealousy.
- I'm feeling blue, meaning feeling down and dispirited.
- That's peachy, meaning it's great.

Each of these sayings conjures up a slightly different shade of color. Whatever shade you imagine is right for you as there are no rights or wrongs, and whatever colors are there are for you to interpret your own way.

Colors also have different meanings in different cultures. For example, in Western cultures it's common to wear black as a color of mourning, while in India white is the color of mourning. In the West brides usually wear white, while in India they wear red. Different colors have different meanings in different cultures, so it's extremely important to know exactly what each color means to you.

Generally Accepted Meanings of Colors

Because your feelings about colors are possibly and even probably influenced by your culture, let's take a look at what colors are typically taken to mean in the West and around the world.

PRIMARY COLORS

A primary color is a color in its own right. It is not made up of any colors other than itself, and when mixed with another primary color, it creates other colors.

RED

Red is the color of love and passion, and men give women red roses to show their love. In India red is the color of marriage and prosperity. Wedding dresses are red, only married women wear red saris, and money is given away in red envelopes. Red is also the color of blood, anger, passion, fire, action, and fever, as we know from phrases such as "he is red in the face."

Red is also a warning color, as in red traffic lights and road signs the world over. In spiritual terms, red is a color of creation and manifestation for when we start with ideas, they feel right, and we take action to manifest them in the real world. Red therefore has a lot to do with our sense of security and physical well-being.

Red in an aura is often an indication of inflammation, whether it be an inflamed mood or an actual infection within the body. Its location within the aura will give a clue as to what problems may be festering. For instance, if red is found near a person's forehead, then perhaps they have a headache or have suffered a brain injury. More about this in chapter 7.

YELLOW

Yellow is the color of the sun, of joy, optimism, imagination, intellect, and analysis. All around the world, it's considered to be a happy color. In Germany yellow represents envy, whereas in Egypt it conveys good fortune. It can, however, also indicate cowardice such as in the phrase "he is yellow," or sickliness, such as the yellowish pallor of jaundice and other illnesses. It's the color of feelings and thus carries our emotions and energy.

Yellow in an aura is often a reflection of a person's intellect and curiosity as well as how emotional they may be.

BLUE

Blue is the color of the sea and the sky, and in most places is thought to be a calm and peaceful color representing trust and security. It's said to be the color of protection. In the Middle East many people wear blue jewelry to ward off evil. Blue is associated with communication and peace. It's also seen as the color of mild depression and low moods, as in the phrase "feeling blue." Some people also see blue as a healing color and a color of peace.

A lot of blue in an aura can indicate the person is a good communicator, whereas turquoise can be an indication of coming change.

Black and White

Let's look at the other major colors associated with auras starting with black and white. Just the phrase "black and white" indicates the extreme paradox of opposites, but it also can mean clarity such as "there it is in black and white." As we have said, colors are neither positive nor negative—they are just what they are and mean different things to different people. Their meanings to you are entirely dependent on how they make you feel.

BLACK

Black is made up of all the primary colors mixed together in equal quantities. As soon as you mix more of one with another, you will get a slightly different shade; hence we talk about blue black, brown black, red black, and so on. There are said to be 105 different shades of black. All these are black, but each is subtly different and open to different interpretations.

In the West, black usually represents depression and sickness. It often indicates a long-term lack of forgiveness toward the self or another. If collected in a specific part of the aura, black can indicate health challenges and unreleased grief. Where the black is within the aura may well indicate the emotional issue it's attached to, so black in the ovaries could indicate unprocessed grief from a miscarriage or the loss of a parent at a young age.

It's important to remember that black is not just a negative color. In many cultures black symbolizes sophistication and formality. In the Middle East black represents rebirth, and in Africa it symbolizes age, maturity, and masculinity. Black is not associated with any specific energy center, although shades of black or gray within chakras will be reflected in the aura and do indicate physical, emotional, mental, or spiritual blockages.

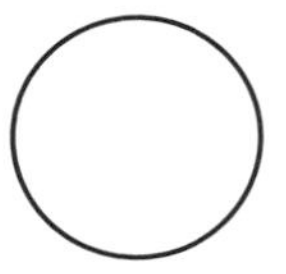

WHITE

White is made up of all the colors of the rainbow mixed together. It's pure light, and as such in Western cultures it represents purity and truth. It allows other colors to be set off against it, so it is neutral. It can indicate enlightenment, meditation, and spiritual qualities. In China, Korea, India, and some other Asian countries, however, white represents death and mourning, and it is traditionally worn at funerals. In Peru, white is associated with good health and angels.

In an aura, white can have many different meanings, and with practice your senses and intuition will tell you the meaning. White sparkles or flashes of white light in the aura may show that a person is pregnant or that they soon will be. Babies often have a white aura. White in an aura can also indicate a spirit guide being close by.

Like black, white is not associated with any specific energy center, but as the combination of all the colors of the rainbow, it's often seen around the heads of spiritual and enlightened people. White as a mixture of all colors can be added to any color to change the shade and make it lighter, and this will also change its energy.

Secondary Colors and Shades of Colors

As soon as you start mixing together the primary colors, you combine the energies and meanings of those colors. If you mix two primary colors in equal proportions, you get the secondary colors, but if you mix them in different proportions, you get shades of colors. Let's go through these colors in the approximate order you'd find them in the rainbow.

VERMILLION

(Yellow-red) irritated, energetic, hurried

CRIMSON
(Blue-red) passionate, angry

STRAWBERRY RED
Rash or fever

TOMATO RED
Rage

LIGHT BRIGHT PINK
Joy, love, warmth, compassion, new or revived romance, self-respect, healthy blood supply, rosy, innocent, feminine, blushing, baby girls

DARK PINK
Immature or dishonest nature

MAGENTA
Unconditional love, grace, deep healing, the higher heart chakra, connection to higher dimensions

MAROON
Masculine, earthy, sensual, hidden motives

ORANGE
Orange is a secondary color, the mixture of red and yellow. It combines the physical energies of red—groundedness, security, and manifestation—with the emotional and intellectual energies of yellow. Orange is often thought of as a color of sunshine, warmth, harvest, and autumn leaves. Connected to our reasons for being here from both a physical and emotional perspective, it governs our sexuality, fertility,

self-expression, imagination, creativity, and growth. It often represents an extremely artistic person of great pride, passion, and emotion. It's often indicative of psychic ability. In Asia, orange is a sacred color worn by Hindu and Buddhist monks. Within an aura, it can also indicate someone who is developing psychic ability.

CORAL

Coral is a living organism that grows very slowly but is extremely hard and brittle. It grows attached to rocks or other corals, so it is seen as representing community spirit.

LIGHT OR PALE YELLOW

Positive excitement about new ideas

BRIGHT LEMON YELLOW

Struggling to maintain power and control in a personal or business relationship; fear of losing control, prestige, respect, or power

BRIGHT GOLD

Intellectual, happy, spiritual energy, and power activated and awakened, an inspired person, a color often seen around babies

DARK YELLOW OR DARK GOLD

Struggling with studies, overly analytical to the point of feeling fatigued or stressed, trying to make up for lost time by learning everything at once

GREEN

Green is the secondary color created when blue and yellow are mixed, and as such it carries much of the energies of both the primary colors. Green is primarily seen as a healing color, a color of calm, balance, nurturing, tranquility, and teaching, as well as being the color of nature and spring. It's also the color of money, so it represents abundance and good luck. It can, however, also be seen as jealousy (the green-eyed monster), envy, smothering, and being overly responsible. In Mexico green is the national color that stands for independence, while in the Middle East green represents fertility and is considered the traditional color of Islam. In Asia and the West, it represents youth, as with the phrase "he is a bit green" meaning inexperienced, whereas in China no man would wear a green hat because it means his wife has been unfaithful.

EMERALD GREEN

Green in an aura is often representative of a healer (maybe a professional healer, a natural healer, or one who is unaware of their healing abilities), and healing hands usually have an emerald green aura around the fingertips. It also indicates a loving and usually demonstrative person.

LIGHT GREEN

Tranquility, harmony

LIME GREEN

Leadership

JADE GREEN

Wisdom, abundance

FOREST GREEN

Jealousy, resentment, feeling like a victim, blaming self and others, insecurity, low self-esteem, inability to understand personal responsibilities, sensitive to things that are seen as criticism

LIGHT BLUE

Intuitive, expressive, truthful, may enjoy a career involving communication

ROYAL BLUE

Clairvoyant, highly spiritual, generous, on the right path, new opportunities coming

DARK BLUE

Fear of the future, fear of self-expression, fear of facing or speaking the truth

TURQUOISE

This is a shade of blue and green, and it is associated with communication and inner truth. It's expansive, expressive, avant-garde, and risk-taking. It is associated with networking, travel, exotic places, freedom, restlessness, initiating energy, and an interest in language. It often indicates a time of transition and change. In the ancient world it was the color of wealth and opulence. Turquoise as in the stone has been used by many cultures both ancient and modern to ward off evil and to protect. In ancient Egypt it was a symbol of transition and rebirth. In the Tibet region of China it's often worn by the general public and by monks, because it signifies not only the cycle of life, death, and rebirth but also the development of wisdom through reincarnation, which is central to Buddhism. Many people see it as color of transition, beginnings, and endings. Wearing the color turquoise or the turquoise gemstone reputedly opens the heart and enhances spirituality, encouraging the individual to identify and speak their truth. Being a shade of blue and green, it's associated with both the heart and the throat chakra.

PURPLE

This color is traditionally associated with royalty, as only kings and queens could wear purple robes. In Japan the highest-ranked monks wore purple. In the Catholic Church it's associated with faith, piety, and penitence. It's also the color of honor, as in the American medal the Purple Heart. It's associated with spiritual guidance and transformation, luck, charm, clairvoyance, and mysticism.

COBALT

Theatrical, ambitious

CLEAR OR BRIGHT PURPLE

In tune with the divine spiritual realm, enlightenment, and claircognizance (the ability to psychically know things)

DARK PURPLE

A cry for love and attention, arrogance, and ambition

REDDISH VIOLET

Clairaudience (the ability to hear the voice of the higher self, God, angels, ascended masters, or spirit guides)

INDIGO

Indigo is often associated with intuition, spirituality, and psychic awareness. People with mainly indigo auras can be intense, idealistic, deep thinking with deep feelings. They can be reserved and lonely, with a tendency to be rigid in their thinking. There are many children and young adults known today as *indigo children* because there is so much indigo in their auras. They tend to think and behave differently than others and move outside of the expected norm, which implies the breaking of the norm and moving to the next level. They are often labeled as having Asperger syndrome or autism because their brains function differently than the majority. They are highly intelligent, and many believe they are the forerunners of a significant change within humans, such as the change from *Homo erectus* to *Homo sapiens*. In the Bible, indigo is indicative of heavenly grace.

VIOLET

Violet is associated with our connection to the greater universe and universal energy. Violet is said to represent religious devotion, imagination, and dreams. When the crown chakra is open, it connects us to our spiritual selves, to our connection with the greater cosmos, and to the divine within ourselves and God. The color is also calming. Violet in an aura often shows a deeply religious person. It can also indicate someone who has few boundaries. Babies often have a lot of violet in their auras because the fontanelle at the crown of their heads is still open.

LAVENDER

Lavender is associated with people who have higher vibrations. It represents purity, beauty, femininity, devotion, serenity, and grace. It brings tranquility, inner peace, and connection to higher dimensions. It is rarely seen in auras.

GOLD

Intuition, self-knowledge, cleansing, psychic gifts, joy, wisdom, abundance

SILVER

Ability to astral travel, unity, strong psychic powers, clarity, abundance

BRIGHT METALLIC

Receptive to new ideas, intuitive, and nurturing

DARK GRAY

This color denotes boredom, malaise, and masking fear or emotion. Residue of fear is accumulating in the body and that can bring bad health. This is especially true if you see gray clustered in specific areas of the body. If this is the only color in the aura, the person is likely to die within a week or two!

Tip

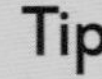

Rainbow stripes or what looks like sunbeams radiating from the person can indicate a lucky person or just someone who is in their first incarnation on earth.

Colors Are Neutral

Even with all of the meanings associated with colors around the world and through the ages, colors in themselves are neither good nor bad. They are expressions of energy, nothing more. Colors mixed with black are not bad, and those mixed with white are not necessarily more spiritual. Pure white is often seen as the most spiritual color because it's all the colors mixed together, but in many cultures, white is the color of mourning. A very pale color in an aura can mean the person is vibrating at higher frequencies, but it can also suggest that the person is being noncommittal. Pink could register as a wishy-washy attitude to relationships, or it could signify a more highly evolved person whose heart chakra is vibrating at the frequency of unconditional love.

Color interpretation is a subtle skill that grows with practice, and there are lots of things you can do to expand your awareness of what colors mean to you. You will learn more from personal experience than you ever will from reading about the experiences of others, and the following exercises will help you gain those experiences. It is important to approach them without worrying about whether you are right or wrong, because there is no right or wrong; whatever you experience is exactly right for you at this moment in time.

EXERCISE 1
WALK WITH AWARENESS

The next time you're out for a walk, notice the colors in nature, the different shades of green, blue, brown, red, yellow, and so on. Notice how each of them makes you feel. This is important because these feelings are the first things that you will notice most when you start to see auras and to interpret them. Notice how they combine to make differing shades and how those differing shades affect your mood, because that is reflected in your aura.

EXERCISE 2
COLORS OF THE HOME

Notice the different colors in your home. Ask yourself why you decorated each room with those colors. What were you aiming to achieve? Notice how being in each room affects the way you feel, because those feelings will be reflected in your aura. Notice also how over the years you have changed the colors you use in your home. How did that reflect your life at that time?

EXERCISE 3
THE COLORS OF YOUR CLOTHES

Notice the color of the clothes in your wardrobe. Notice how your mood is affected by the color of the clothes you choose to wear. Notice why you may prefer some colors over others on different days and how the colors affect you, because those colors affect your aura, and your aura sends subtle signals to others that determine the way in which they experience you. Have your favorite colors changed over the years?

EXERCISE 4
PICTURE THE COLORS

Relax with a few slow breaths and visualize a cloud of color. Imagine yourself breathing it in and it traveling around your body. How does it make you feel? Then imagine breathing in a different color and notice how that feels. The most important thing is how each color makes you feel, because colors need to have meaning for you. Everyone is different, and everyone will interpret colors slightly differently. For example, some people see black as a negative color that makes them feel uneasy whereas others see it as a safe color. Neither is right neither is wrong—it's just what it is for you.

EXERCISE 5
DIVINING THE SUBTLE

Once you have practiced interpreting what colors mean to you, you can work on reading them in auras. Gather an assortment of objects in different colors, such as a variety of leaves, flowers, and trinkets from around your home. Also gather fabrics in different colors, such as scarves, shirts, and tea towels.

Pick the objects up one by one and look at them carefully. Notice the color and the texture and how they make you feel. Pick up something in a similar color and notice the subtle difference. Continue noticing the subtle differences between the similar colors and the more obvious differences between major color changes. Now wrap one of the colored objects in a piece of material of a different color and then hold them both. What do you feel from the two combined textures and colors?

What You'll Learn

The purpose of these exercises is to give you a greater depth in your interpretations of the different colors so that when you reach the point of reading auras and healing auras, you will understand what you are seeing and feeling. One day, you will pass your hands through someone else's aura, and you will recall what you felt while doing these exercises.

For instance, if you wrapped a silver knife in a pink blouse and it gave you a certain feeling, then one day while passing your hands through an aura you recall the same feeling, or the same image pops into your mind, then whatever you felt during the exercise will be what you needed to know about the aura. From there, every time you see a combination of silver and pink in the aura, you will begin to work out whether the event was in the past or if it is happening now. Also whether it is a physical, emotional, mental, or spiritual issue. For me, it might indicate that the person whose aura I am feeling needs to let something go or have something unpleasant taken away from them. They may need to break away from a toxic relationship, or it could be more physical. They may have a heart operation scheduled for the near future, or they may already have had one.

7

AURA READING

As we have previously discussed, in one way or another everyone unconsciously senses and reads auras. Psychics spend a lot of time and energy developing their senses and practicing their skills, and some psychics, particularly clairvoyants who *see* things, specialize in aura reading. What they are doing is noticing the colors in an aura—the depth and shades of the colors and the positions of the colors within the aura. The aura holds all the information about the subject—the past, present, and what the near future is bringing—so these spiritual workers are able to "read" the individual and give information that the subject themselves may not be consciously aware of.

What an Aura Reading Can Tell You

By having an aura reading, you can discover your predominant color, which will tell you a lot about how you operate on an unconscious level. It will reveal the patterns of thought and behavior that may be holding you back. It will reveal your strengths and weaknesses, so you can play to those strengths and achieve your goals. If you're not sure what your goals are, then the colors in your aura will guide you toward the type of career that is going to make you happiest. It can even guide you toward people you will get along well with. Many people have an aura reading to discover what type of person is going to be best suited to them as a life partner, because as with everything else, some colors go better together than others.

The colors in our auras also reflect our moods, our emotions, our feelings, our worries, and our fears, which obviously are constantly changing. As we grow, we change, and the predominant color of our aura will change. Most of us, however, develop our life-long personalities throughout childhood, and childhood events mold us and are reflected in our predominant aura color. It represents our basic personality. That's why a baby's aura is often white or rainbow colored, because it is ready to reflect what they become. When a psychic is doing an aura reading, they focus on all the different levels of the aura and the colors within each level.

How to Discover Your Predominant Aura Color

There is a very simple and effective way of discovering your predominant aura color and that of others.

- Settle yourself comfortably in front of a mirror and take a few deep breaths to ensure you're relaxed. Soften your gaze and stare at your reflection for a minute or two, focusing on the area between the head and the shoulder. At this point you may well see a heat haze and color around your reflection. If so, you're seeing your own aura.

Tip

The same exercise can be used to see the auras of others, just without the mirror.

- If you don't see anything, continue to stare absently at yourself. Let your mind wander, and, after two or three minutes, close your eyes. Against the backdrop of your eyelids, you will see an outline of yourself. What color or colors surround it? This is your aura color at that moment in time, and it usually shows your predominant color.

What Your Predominant Color Means

In aura reading, there are fourteen predominant colors (although some are very rare). So, what does your predominant color say about you (or the person you are looking at)? Remember these descriptions are for your main color. There will be shades of color within your aura that give more range and depth to a full reading, which we will cover later.

Red People

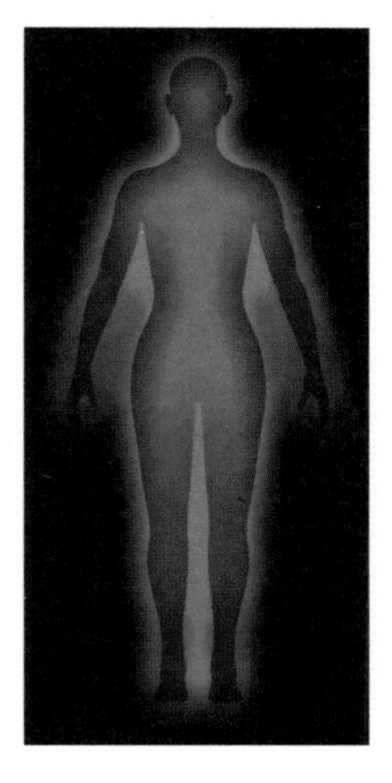

Red people are full of energy and drive. If your aura is predominantly red, then you're sensual, vibrant, passionate, an extrovert, full of enthusiasm, and have a love of life. You have plans and dreams and you have no trouble sharing them. You're more than able to go charging in where angels fear to tread, because you're so enthusiastic about things that are close to your heart. You like new things, new projects, new friends, new clothes, and new adventures. You can get bored easily. You can be quick to anger, but temper tantrums don't last long and are forgotten just as fast. The downside is if things go wrong you can lose confidence in yourself and feel insecure. But you're not down for long and usually bounce back.

You're focused on the present and have little regard for the past and what it can teach you. You are motivated and can keep moving toward your goals, but you can also get easily distracted by things that happen right now.

Your energy and confidence work well for your career. You're noticed, and as long as your confidence does not topple into arrogance, you will do well in fast-moving business such as advertising, marketing, and sales. You would make an excellent entrepreneur and can move mountains when you're passionate about something, which is a lot of the time.

If the color is a darker red, this means you're grounded, attached to the physical plane, and you do not fear physical challenges. If it has tinges of gray or black, there may be strong negative emotions, and you could potentially be getting depressed due to insecurity.

Orange People

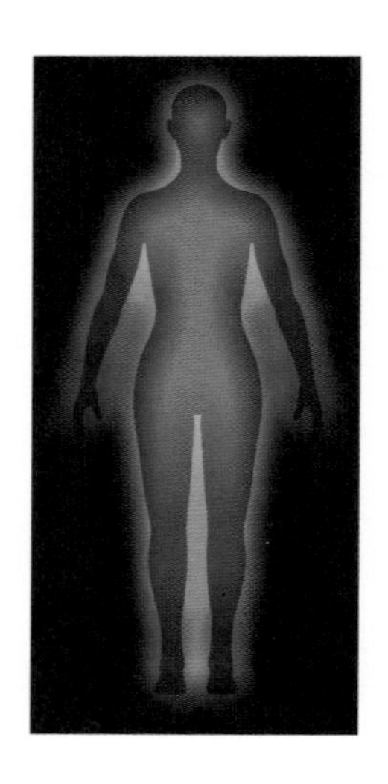

Orange folk are creative and enthusiastic about things they believe in. You can focus on making sure others know how you feel, and you can inspire others to help you move forward. You're compassionate and sensitive to the needs of others. You're a visionary with lots of ideas, and you are able to create a good team dynamic with others who will need to finish your projects while you move quickly on to the next. You enjoy an active and fulfilling social life as well as working hard. You're probably quite athletic as well.

If the orange is the least bit murky, there is a lack of self-worth, insecurity, sluggishness, and a feeling that the sun has gone out of your life.

Yellow People

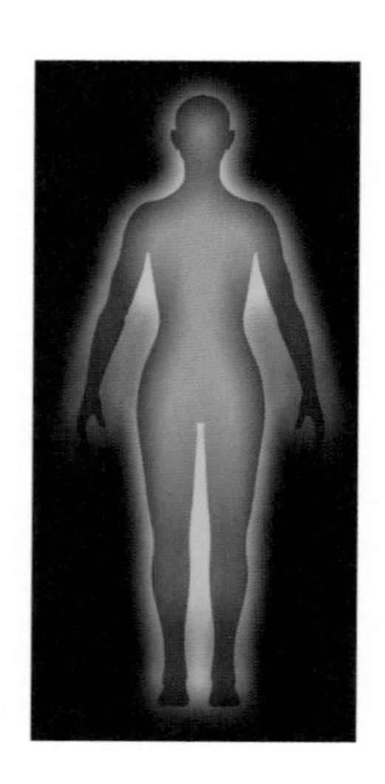

Yellow people are bright, optimistic, intelligent, and energetic. You're sensitive and emotional; you feel things very deeply and can harness your emotions for positive action. You're intuitive and often have a gut reaction to ideas and people. You can be analytical and therefore balance your gut reaction and enthusiasm for action with logical thought to ensure the energy you expend on projects is used to its best advantage. When your intellect and your gut are aligned, you act with confidence and assurance. You have energy and vitality, and like many people of any aura color, but especially for you, when the sun is shining, you automatically respond with a joy of living just for the sake of it. Love and laughter are key at those times.

The darker the yellow, the more cut off you are from your emotions, your instinctive feelings, and other people. You probably spend too much time overanalyzing and prevaricating rather than taking any action.

A tan or brown aura tinge suggests that you're feeling tired because you've taken on too much responsibility. Perhaps you're studying too hard, or perhaps you've taken on responsibilities that are not yours and you're feeling weighed down by them. This indicates that you need to take some time for yourself.

When your aura is turning golden, this shows you're seeking a spiritual pathway and beginning to ask questions about the meaning of life. It also shows that you are trying to clear the issues of the lower chakras and to advance to a higher level.

Green People

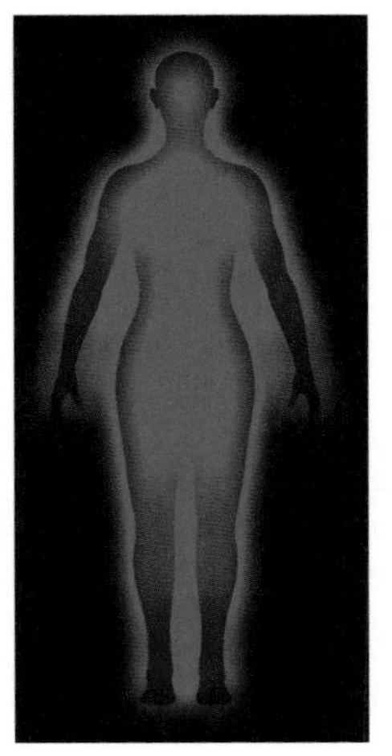

Green people have a strong and commanding presence. You're seen as a healer and counselor, a calm, wise person, and a teacher. Other people can come to you for help and advice. You're empathetic, caring, sensitive, loving, and compassionate. You often put the needs of others before your own. You're self-reliant and independent, and you command respect for yourself and others. You enjoy stimulating, intellectual conversation, and you usually have a great many interests. You're loyal to a fault, but you need to be appreciated.

If you have a muddy or a dark-green aura, you may be possessive and jealous, which are signs of insecurity, and you may be unwilling to accept responsibility for your actions by seeking to blame others. Alternatively, you may have a kind and caring nature that makes you take on too much. If your aura is too dark, you need to start taking care of yourself, because if you don't, you won't be well enough to help others, which is your goal.

Blue People

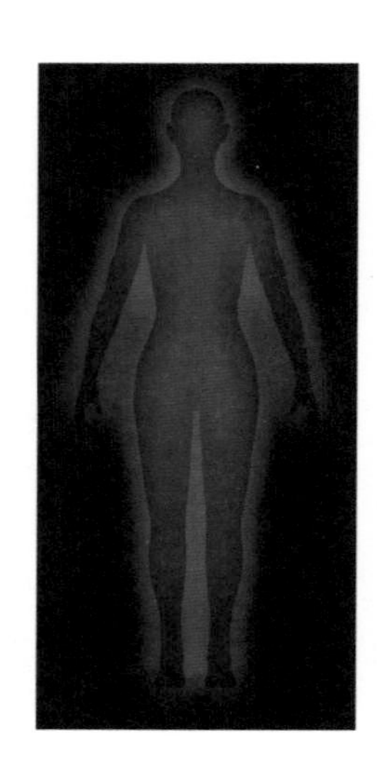

Blue people are seen as generous, honest, calm, and tactful. You exude a sense of peace. People will always be attracted to that energy, and they will come to you when troubled. You're not afraid of speaking your mind or your heart. You have a no-nonsense attitude, and you do not suffer fools gladly, but you do have lots of compassion for those truly in need and you are extremely perceptive. You're intuitive, expressive, and truthful. You find communication easy and may follow a career in some form of communication. You are not judgmental, but you are calm and peaceful, you have plenty of energy, and you can reach out to others and inspire them.

If the blue is dark and murky, you fear expressing yourself, especially of speaking your truth. You may even hide the truth from yourself. You may be suspicious of others, and you may continually need to take charge. Many people suffering from paranoia have a dark, murky-blue aura.

Indigo (Blue-Purple) People

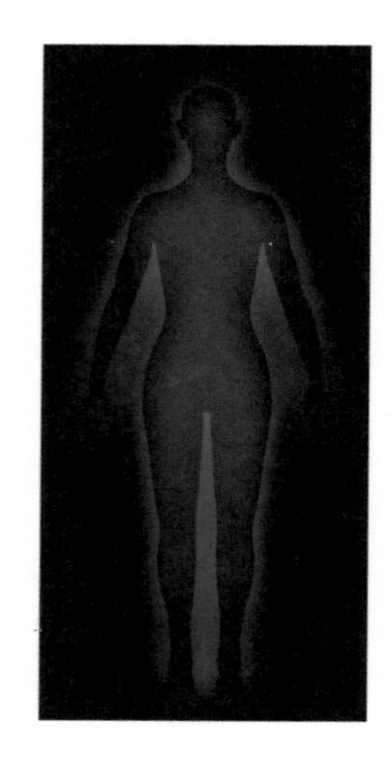

Indigo people are spiritual in varying degrees. There are many shades of purple through to indigo and violet. You can be idealistic and a deep thinker with deep feelings. You're probably seeking the meaning of life. You can sometimes be quite rigid in your thinking. The deeper the purple, the more likely you are to find it difficult to live within society's norms, and you may well try to change things for the better.

Purple in your aura is associated with psychic abilities such as clairvoyance, clairaudience, and, clairsentience. It means you're being guided spiritually toward your higher self. You're likely to be interested in all forms of philosophy. You can sometimes feel you're a fish out of water.

If the aura is a dark and murky purple, it can indicate that you're overly ambitious, attention-seeking, and crying out to be loved. If so, first you must love yourself.

Violet People

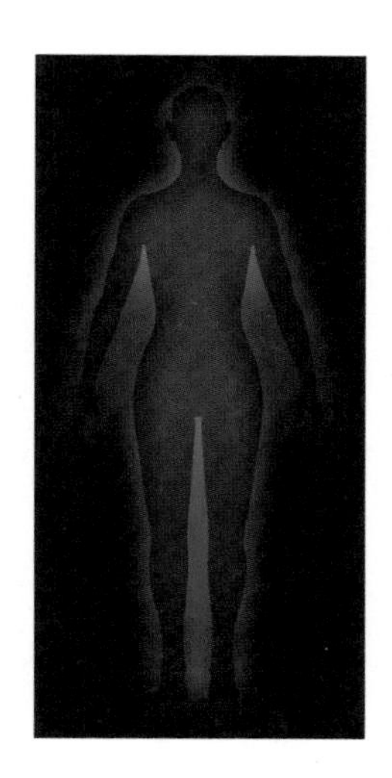

Violet people are connected to the divine. You're extremely imaginative and a creator of dreams, often preferring to be in your imagination than in the real world. You're here to bring unconditional love and to help make the world a better place. Whether you're helping people or animals or the planet itself, your focus is not on yourself but on others.

Everyone has moments of violet in their auras—moments of greatness when they are connected to universal unconditional loving energy, which is the divine. Many violet people are nuns and missionaries, endeavoring to manifest spiritual qualities such as unconditional love, joy, acceptance, and so on into the physical world by "being" spiritual and by making a difference.

Tip

When gray appears in your aura, you may well be bored with life and you're probably burying emotions and fear. Burying emotions takes energy, so you will be tired and listless. Buried emotions and dissatisfaction in life can accumulate in the body and create ailments. The area where the gray is situated in the aura can point in the direction of illnesses that are forming. It means you're out of balance somewhere, and a visit to an energy healer can help you identify the source of your problems.

Black and White People

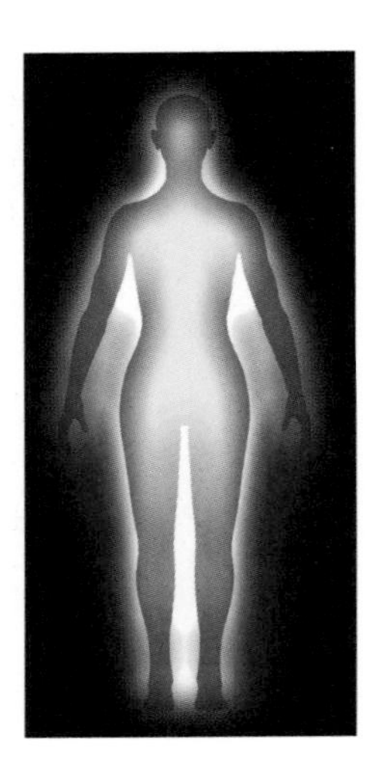

WHITE

White is extremely rare and usually seen only in babies, where there is nothing but pure innocence. If you have a pure white aura, it really means that you're not of this world, you're not grounded, you're totally innocent, and you're probably ready to ascend to a more spiritual state of existence. White in an aura usually is thought to be an angelic being or spirit guide.

BLACK

I have never seen a totally black aura, but black areas are usually indicative of serious illness that may well be caused by a spiritual energy block. If you have just a black spot, then it's identifying an area in the body that is developing a serious physical illness. You probably suppress negative emotions such as anger, envy, resentment, and so forth, and you may have too much on your mind.

Other Colors

Other shades of color appear in many people's auras, and sometimes these can be the predominant color. These colors are blended, pastel, mixed with white, and normally seen as a higher vibration.

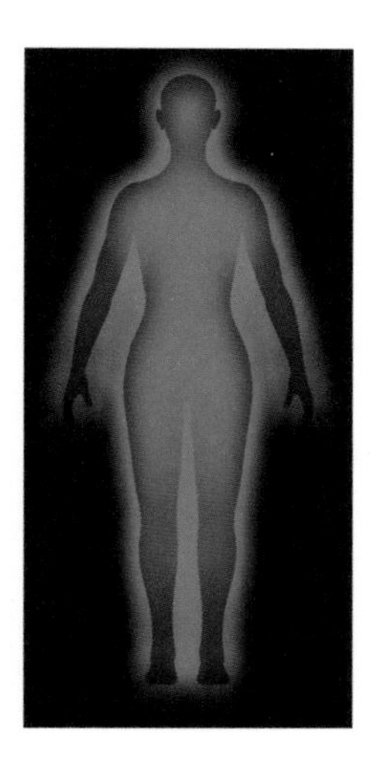

TURQUOISE

Turquoise is similar to blue but at a higher vibration. You're not afraid to express your inner truth. You're good at all forms of communication, you're very expressive, and you can inspire those around you to new heights. You love freedom and travel and are interested in the ancient world, religion, and spirituality. You find energy in tranquility and generally have a positive attitude about life. You're extremely intuitive, and when sitting quietly will receive flashes of inspiration.

A dark, murky turquoise is rarely seen because it would mean that you were deceiving yourself to such a degree that everything you believed yourself to be was a lie. If this happens, a complete reevaluation of your life is in order.

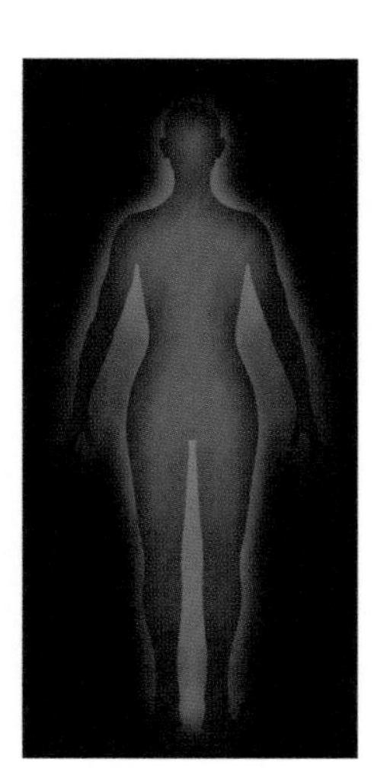

LAVENDER

If you have lavender in your aura, then your crown chakra is open and you're vibrating at a high level. You're a beautiful soul, and it's reflected in your aura. You have a great deal of strength coming from a deep sense of inner peace. You're devoted to your chosen cause and live a life of serenity and grace. You connect easily to the angelic realms.

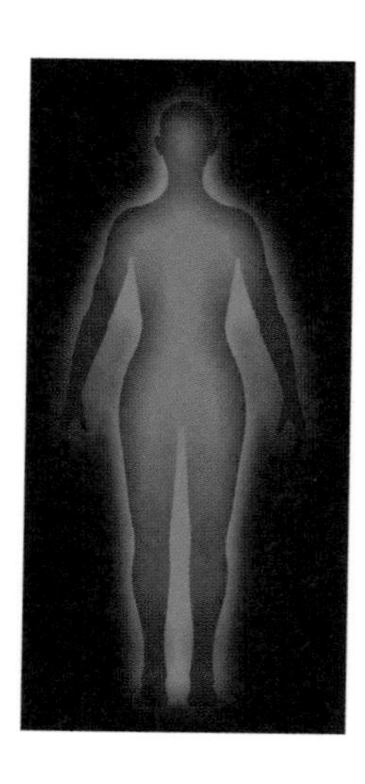

SILVER

If you have silver in your aura, then you have strong psychic powers, and you are able to manage astral travel. Silver is associated with divine feminine energy.

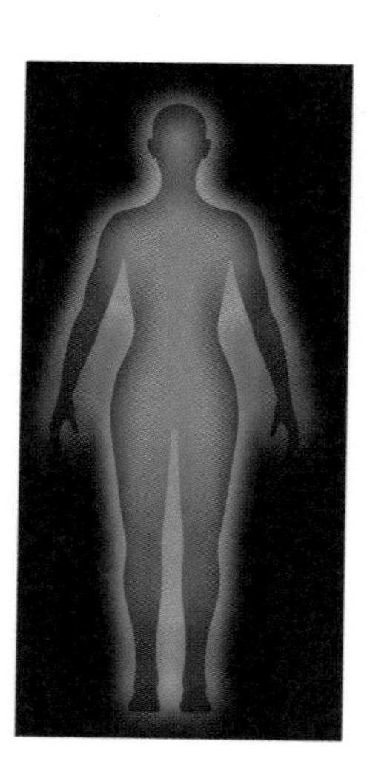

GOLD

A golden aura means you have strong intuitive and psychic abilities. You have worked hard on yourself and have a deep understanding of self. You have developed your healing abilities and your wisdom. You're a secure, happy, joyful person. The healing, nurturing energy you channel is of a very high vibration.

Tip

Should you have rainbows in your aura, then you have a very strong gift for energy healing. All the colors of the rainbow are clear and distinct and balanced, making you a very balanced person.

What the Positions of Colors Mean

There are no hard-and-fast rules about reading auras. It's a very intuitive and personal process, and each aura reader may do things slightly differently than every other. We each tweak our gift and our methods according to what works best for ourselves. The following ideas are the best that I have come across.

When reading an aura, you have to take an overall impression of the major colors, which will give you a good understanding of the person's personality and attitude to life at that particular moment.

For more depth, consider the position of the colors. Generally, the colors on the left of the subject tell you about the person's past, what has been happening, and what is leaving their life. The colors in the middle show what is taking place in the present, and the colors on the right refer to what is coming in the future.

How far a color is from the body will tell you which level of the aura the color is in, that is, if it is a physical, emotional, mental, or spiritual issue.

8

AURAS AND RELATIONSHIPS

We have already looked at the predominant colors of auras, which reflect our outward personalities. No one is going to be all good or all bad or all of one color. We all have some positive as well as negative traits, and of course there is always the influence of other people. The predominant color of someone's aura, however, does give a lot of information about them, and while we know that some colors go together better than others, the same is true of people because some go together better than others. For instance, black and white are opposites, and if mixed together they give varying shades of gray, thus creating a murky black and a murky white. If a person with a predominantly black aura married a person with a predominantly white aura, then a battle for supremacy would be on, and both would become less of themselves.

Obviously, if we work hard on ourselves and release all our blockages, we will raise our vibration, which may well influence and change our overall color. When one partner follows a path of personal and spiritual development and the other doesn't, this can lead to a breakup because they are no longer compatible. Let's now look and see which colors go best together to create harmonious relationships, and which are likely to cause conflict. While the outcome of these pairings is not set in stone, one thing that we can say for sure is that when two people love each other, their auras blend, but somewhere in their combined auras will be shades of pink, which is the color of unconditional love.

What Colors Make Your Best Match?

You can see on a color wheel which colors blend well together.

As with all color theory, primary colors (red, blue, and yellow) go well together. When two primary colors are mixed, they blend easily to create something new and original. (Blending all three together, however, causes murky colors.) This means that the qualities of a red person combined with those of a yellow create a life together that accentuates each of their positive qualities and enables them to live together in the secondary color of orange, and thus in harmony.

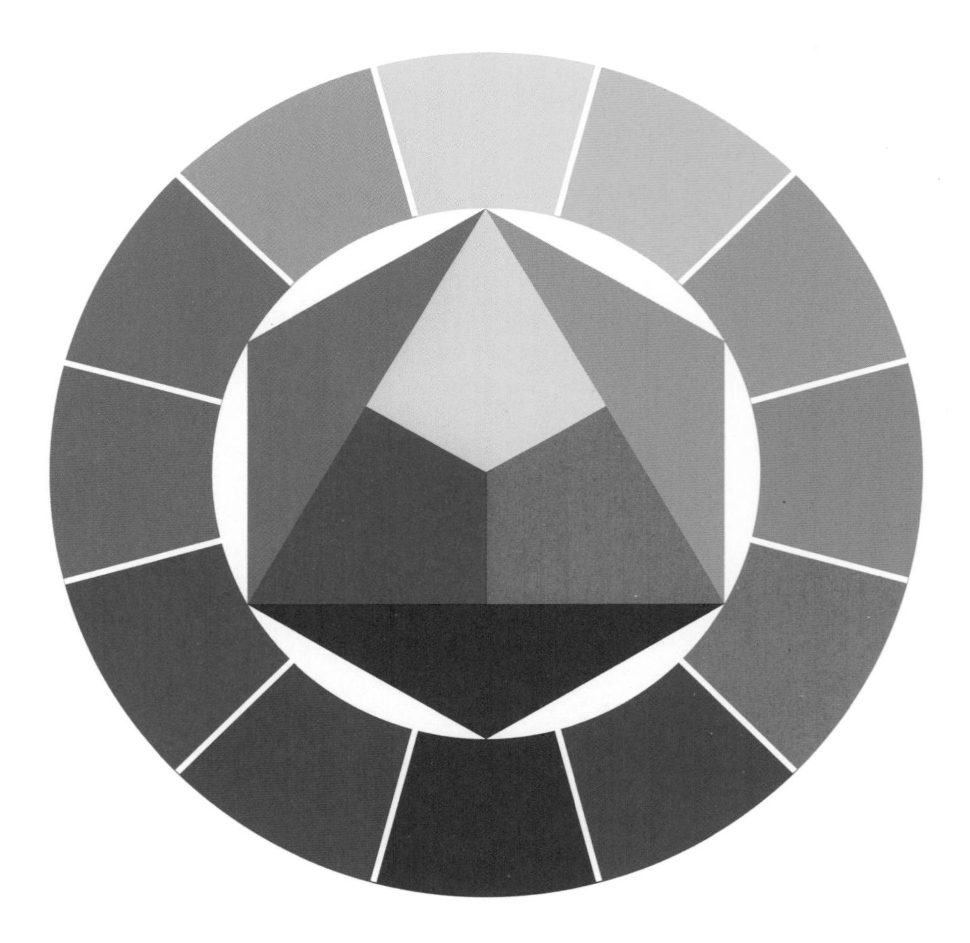

You might assume that red and red would go well together because these people would have so much in common, but in fact they're likely to have much too much energy and would soon be rubbing each other the wrong way. Two passionate, fiery people who are both quick to anger leads to a very volatile relationship. Other less fiery colors can, however, find good relationships with people of their same color. Oranges are well suited to other oranges, and yellows get along great with other yellows.

Matching a secondary color with either of their primary colors that create it makes for a harmonious relationship, because they have similar qualities, so an orange person goes well with a red or yellow person.

Often colors that are very close together can end up causing conflict because their similarities create a fight for dominance, but if they make an effort to love each other, it can work.

We have all heard the expression "opposites attract," and the same is true when looking at the personality types that blend well together in relationships where each partner brings opposite qualities to the relationship. These include:

- Red and green
- Blue and orange
- Yellow and violet

Each individual color has its own strengths and weaknesses when it comes to relationships. The success of a relationship also depends on whether someone is operating from the positive aspects of a color or the negative aspects. Each person is unique, and we are each at a different part of our journey of development. As humans, we seem to believe that we are meant to be in a single relationship for the rest of our lives and we may spend our lives constantly seeking "the one." The truth, however, is that we are souls in the process of development, which makes me wonder why we feel this to be necessary. Few have a single relationship. As teenagers, most of us enter into many relationships while we seek to discover not only who we are but what we want in a relationship. As our auras blend with those of others, we discover who we are compatible with and who doesn't work for us.

Identifying the basic color of a potential partner's aura can save us lots of time. Below are the basic romantic needs of each of the major colors. Read through them and see what color your best match is likely to be.

Reds

Reds have so much energy that physical activity is a must for them, and an active and passionate sex life is essential for their well-being. Because they are volatile, they need a partner who can match their energy and moods, so this has to be someone who can stand up to them without trying to overpower them. Reds are social animals, so their partner must either enjoy an exciting and busy social life or be prepared for their red partner to be involved in a social whirlwind without them. Red may be volatile, but in their opinion, making up is not only the best part of an argument, it's probably the reason for it in the first place.

The best match would probably be an orange person, as long as both red and orange are secure in themselves and there is no jealousy. Green could be another good match for red people, especially if they have common goals. The ambition of the green plus the energy of the red could be an awesome combination, and the impetuousness of the red would be tempered by the common sense of the green.

Oranges

Oranges needs loads of freedom and space just to be. They need time to be alone. This does not mean they do not love their partner; they just need to feel free to be themselves, and they need alone time to recharge their batteries. Orange is extrovert and fun to be around, but they don't like to get too emotionally involved. They need a partner who will understand and support their need for freedom and who will be secure in themselves and able to offer support without clinging or overpowering.

The best match would be another orange because they would be able to respect each other's need for space and to be themselves. Alternatively, the ambition of the relaxing green would harness the orange energy without overpowering it, and they would both be able to relax in each other's company.

Yellows

Yellows need to have fun, so their partner must be their playmate as well as lover. They are very optimistic, creative, and need to be able to spend time pursuing their particular brand of creativity. They prefer intellectual conversations ranging over many subjects, their minds are eager, and they constantly learn and try things out. They are lighthearted, witty, and flirtatious. If connected to their feelings, they will be expressive and expansive, but the majority have their feelings well in check, and may not even be consciously aware of some of the raw emotions that lie beneath their lively and extroversive personalities. They can be quite vulnerable, but they are unlikely to show it. They need a partner who will be gentle, kind, and supportive. They will seek to please their partner and may well need constant reassurance. If they receive criticism instead, they may well just give up. They need a partner who will love them as they *are* rather than as the person they may be trying to become.

The best match would be another yellow because this would be a stimulating and highly sexual relationship. Both colors need space, freedom, and trust based on honesty. As long as they both get this, there won't be any problems. What keeps them together is the mutual need for deep emotional ties within a relationship of freedom and trust.

Greens

Greens have a very practical attitude toward their relationships and life. Things need to be fun, but they often keep their feelings hidden. Greens are usually balanced, intelligent, and ambitious, so they are often found in the business world. They are enthusiastic, very loyal, and want their partnership to be successful, so they will work hard at making it so. Unfortunately, greens blend with many other colors, so they may begin to take on their partner's energy and color, which makes them change from being their own selves while they do their best to adapt to their partner's energy. The longer they are together, the more like their partner they will become. Forming and adhering to boundaries can be difficult for them. As natural healers, they want to help others and often forget to identify their *own* needs and to help themselves or to ask for help when they need it.

The best match would be pink. Pink and green are both full of love, although green is more practical while pink is a dreamer. If they agree with each other in their dreams, then they will work well together. Alternatively, orange would be able to relax with green and the pragmatism of green would keep orange in check without being overpowering.

Pinks

Pinks are romantic, tender, and dreamy, and they truly believe that their dreams will come true. They see the best in people, and they won't allow anyone to point out that the person of their affections may not be who they think they are, so they can get hurt. They see life and love through rose-colored glasses, and when the glasses are forcibly removed, they can be easily crushed. They are optimistic, however, and they usually bounce back and put the rose-colored glasses back in place, because otherwise the world would be just too awful for their kind and loving hearts to cope with. They need a partner who is just as romantic as they are, and who shares their dreams. As long as they have some practicality in their nature, they may even be able to make the dreams come true.

The best match is green, but another good one is turquoise. Pink and turquoise would be totally infatuated with each other as long as neither found a flaw in the other, and this is unlikely, as flaws would be brushed under the proverbial carpet. Neither is particularly ambitious, so they would get along well together in their own rosy paradise.

Blues

Blues need total commitment. They are very sensitive, caring souls who crave complete intimacy with their partners. If they have connected to their deeper feelings, then they communicate with ease and will expect the same in return. If they have not, then they will expect their partner to "know" how they feel—while they assume they "know" how their partner feels—without having to express things openly. Of course, these assumptions are often wrong and can lead to plenty of misunderstandings. Blues need partners who can express their emotions and feelings sensitively and openly.

The best match is yellow, as long as neither is the jealous kind, because that would kill the relationship. Yellow has emotion, energy, and a free spirit, while blue is calm, peaceful, and healing. If the two are well balanced as people, they should have a successful relationship. Alternatively, there is turquoise. Both blue and turquoise are linked to communication, so turquoise will ensure they have deep and meaningful conversations and will encourage blue to express their feelings. Together they will be very relaxed; not much will ruffle them, and they will live in harmony.

Turquoises

Turquoises love an open, honest, and easy-going relationship in which they can feel relaxed. Trust is important to turquoise, as well as beauty, humor, and intellectual interaction. Turquoise can be idealistic, but they can become very dispirited when their expectations are not met. Integrity is very important to turquoise, so they need a partner who is going to express themselves clearly and who is always there for them. When let down, they find it hard to forgive, but they take lessons to heart and grow through their experiences rather than holding grudges. They take responsibility, move on, and share their experiences with others. Turquoise is about transforming negative experiences into positive ones, so they won't tolerate a partner who sees themselves as a victim.

The best match is another turquoise because both are sensitive and tender. They communicate on the same level and are quite carefree. They both prefer to go with the flow of life, so not having any particular goals suits both of them. They may each be a little vulnerable but, owing to their mutual sensitivity and ability to communicate, there are few misunderstandings and a lot of mutual support.

Violets

Violet people love to daydream. They are very intuitive and artistic, and they have very active imaginations. They love to float among the clouds, so they find the hard realities of life difficult to cope with. If someone hurts them, they become the proverbial "once bitten twice shy," and they will take a very long time to trust again or to share their feelings. Love and sex go hand in hand for them, and so sex for its own sake is an anathema to them. They also have surprisingly dynamic personalities and can make great leaders because they are visionaries who inspire others with their inner strength and confidence. Violets need a partner who understand their wildest dreams and who can soar to great heights with them, so their partners need to be their equals.

The best match is another violet. They will see each other as soul mates, and they will hate to be apart. They will be in constant communication wherever in the world each of them may be. They are so totally absorbed in each other that they may cut themselves off from the rest of the world. They will be totally focused on making their dreams reality.

Indigos

Indigo people are deeply spiritual people who are here to set an example for others. They live spiritual lives in line with their soul's purpose. They are fiercely independent and won't be bound by society's standards, nor will they allow themselves to be pigeonholed in any particular behavior or group. Peer pressure is not something indigos submit to. They will go their own way, setting an example for how to live a spiritual life, because they have already learned to love unconditionally and have long since let go of judgment, shame, and guilt. This does not mean that they just go with the flow; it means they have strong beliefs that they live by.

The best match for an indigo person would be another indigo because they would respect each other and have an intuitive understanding. Violets and blues are also very good choices. Red would be good as well, although both partners would have strong views and would probably have to agree to disagree on some things.

Lavenders

Lavender people are deeply intuitive, gentle, and caring free spirits. Their senses are highly developed, so they see the energies of others and connect to them. They can be deeply vulnerable because their imagination knows no bounds. Lavenders need to be free to explore the world while maintaining gentle, caring relationships. They are acutely aware of their spiritual natures and not only have a lot of unconditional love to share but also need to receive it. Their spirits need to be free to express themselves, share their love, and try to make the world a better place. They can, however, get very discouraged at times and need love and support to get them back on their feet.

The best match could be another violet due to the free and easy rapport they would have with each other. They will feel they have met before in previous lives—and they probably have. As long as they both respect the other's dreams and spiritual desires, they should have a deeply rewarding, lifelong relationship.

Whites

If someone has a pure white aura, then they are vibrating at a level that is probably not of this world, and the chances of them being in a relationship are very low. They are more likely to be monks and nuns and to be living a life devoted to some kind of spiritual pursuit. If they are in a relationship it will be with either a magenta or pink, both of whom would be loving and gentle.

Silvers

Silver is the color of purity and innocence and is often seen in the auras of young children. In adults it's associated with people who have exceptional psychic powers, a strong belief in the unity of humankind, animals, planets, and the universe, and they have a deep connection to their inner divine feminine intuitive energy regardless of their gender. If the aura is bright, then they are very receptive to new ideas and have a deeply nurturing disposition. This color aura is also associated with astral travel.

Best matches for silver are lavenders or pinks because of their very sensitive natures. Turquoise and indigo could also be possibilities. Gold would be excellent as they are also spiritually aligned.

Golds

Gold usually signifies an activated and awakened spiritual energy. It's the color of great wisdom and learning. It's a high vibrational color and connects to the higher dimensions, and therefore not seen very often. It is representative of the divine masculine energy of the universe. Silver is a good match for gold, as are the other gentle and spiritual colors, including violet, indigo, and green.

A Summary of Matches

To sum up, here are some of the colors that may go well together are:

Color	Matches
Reds	yellows, greens, oranges
Oranges	reds, yellows, oranges, blues, greens
Magentas	reds, blues, whites
Pinks	reds, whites, blues, magentas, greens
Yellows	yellows, reds, blues, greens, oranges
Green	blues, yellows, oranges, pinks, violets
Blues	yellows, reds, blues, violets, indigos
Violets	reds, greens, blues, yellows, violets, indigos, turquoises, lavenders
Indigos	blues, violets, indigos, reds
Lavenders	violets, silvers, golds, turquoises
Silvers	turquoises, lavenders, pinks, indigos
Golds	yellows, silvers, violets, indigos, greens, magentas

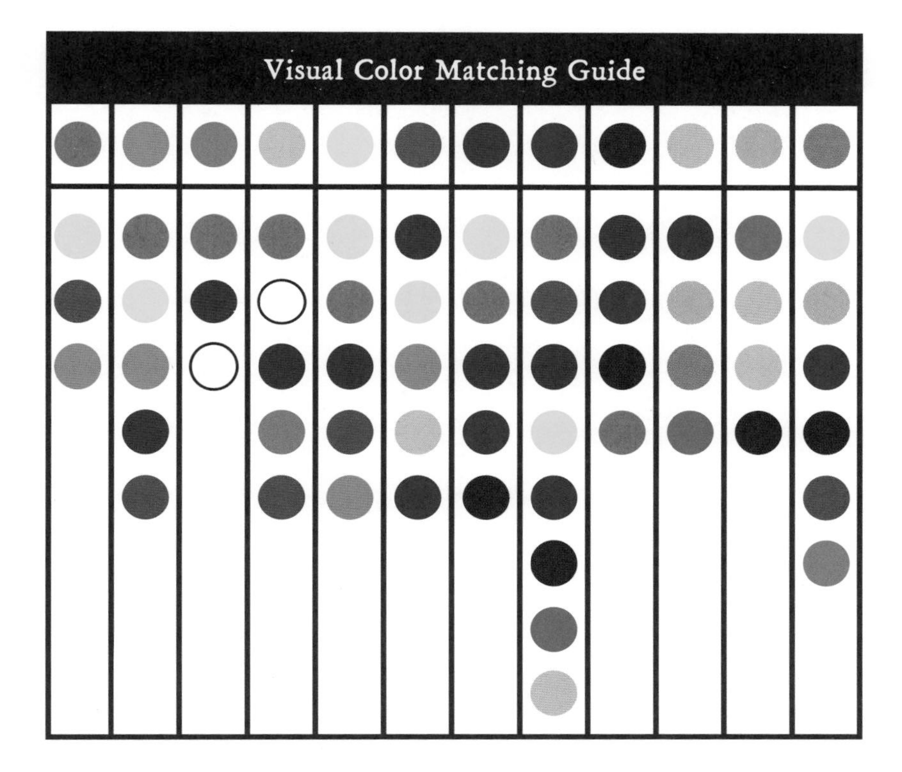

This doesn't mean you can't have a good relationship with someone who is not listed as a color you are likely to get along with, but it may mean you have to work harder at it. There will always be other issues in the mix as well, so trust your instincts and be prepared to accept the way that others are and be happy. If not, check out your auras to see what's going on and take it from there.

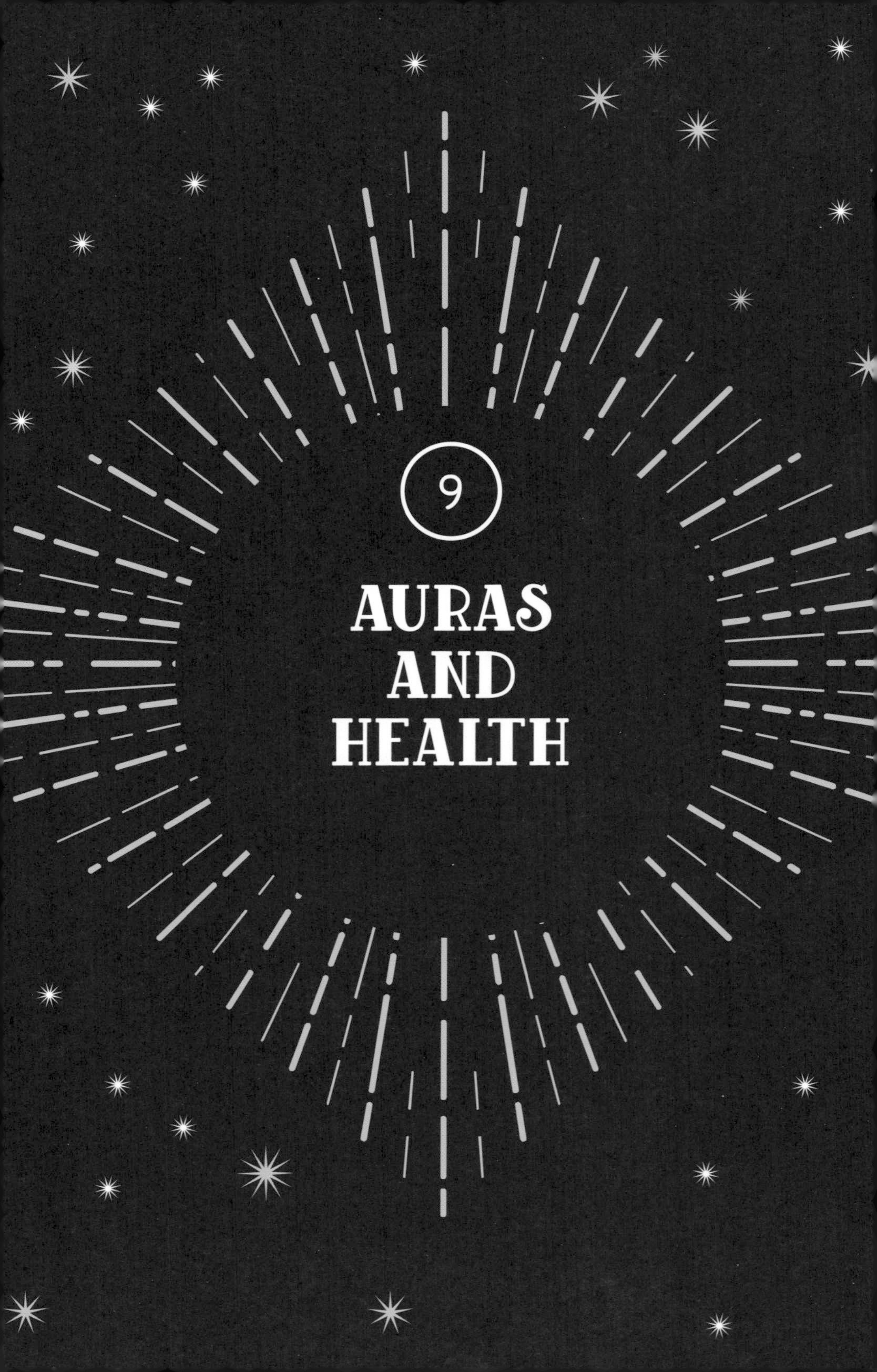

9

AURAS AND HEALTH

Moods, emotions, and health may affect the aura in different ways. Our aura reflects everything about us at one moment in time. It reflects our physical, emotional, mental, and spiritual well-being. It reflects everything we have ever learned and whether we are living in line with our soul's purpose. If we are happy and healthy, we have a happy- and healthy-looking aura. It will be bright and shining, and we will feel energized. If we are tired and lethargic, then our aura will reflect this by being anything from not very bright to positively dull. It may have dark or smudgy patches within it or even a tear.

Equally, we can lift our mood and energy by brightening and strengthening our aura. Simple things can make a big difference, such as taking a trip to a park or an outdoor space; getting some exercise such as walking, running, or swimming; or meeting a friend for a chat. But there are much quicker and easier ways to brighten the aura. Eating a healthy snack such as a piece of fresh fruit will help, as will having flowers around the house or in your workplace. Taking five minutes to look out of the office window at something natural or pretty will make a difference. Focusing on your breathing for a minute while stuck in traffic will make you feel better and brighten your aura.

Tip

If you're feeling tired and stressed, just sit outdoors for five minutes and it will make you feel better, or spend five minutes staring at water, whether it be the sea, a river, a pond, a fountain, or even a birdbath—it will leave you feeling more relaxed and positive as well as brightening and energizing your aura. When you find yourself stuck and unable to find the answer to a problem or project, go to a window and look out at the sky for a moment. Watching the shapes the clouds make may help ideas to flow again.

How Colors Give Indications of Health

Early indications of illnesses can begin to appear within the aura. The aura is a reflection of a person's energy, and if a person feels down, the aura may reflect this by being dull and lifeless, but that doesn't mean nothing can be done. With a transference of energy either via an energy healer or a positive boost of energy into the aura from some natural source, the aura is lifted and so is the person. Whenever you are feeling unwell or know that you are sick or have a medical condition, you should always see a doctor. The work that can be done with your aura is not a substitution for medical screenings or treatment, but it can work as a complementary therapy alongside those practices to help facilitate healing.

When someone is ill, dull, gray, or black patches may appear and disappear as thoughts flit through their mind. Color can fade, or, as in the example shown here, red angry-looking patches can form, indicating ailments such as sinusitis or a sore throat. The positions of these patches or low energy areas show where potential problems may be forming. Knowing this allows people to rebalance their lives and seek medical attention to potentially nip illnesses in the bud.

Colors in the aura can also indicate emotional or spiritual unwellness. A very dark base chakra within the aura is also an indication of deep insecurity issues. The turquoise at the base and the top of the image also indicates a transition, so perhaps this person is going to start letting go of their insecurity and step forward in a new and positive frame of mind. There is violet on the far-right edge, indicating a more spiritual perspective is coming.

The Healing Tree

There are a myriad complementary therapies, such as reiki, shamanism, and the aura healing I talk about in this book. They come from around the world and are available for people to connect with and learn from, depending upon their own belief system. Though they seem different, I believe they all come from the same source that could be seen as a tree. The seed is planted. We can't see it, and we probably don't know it is there until it begins to grow. As it grows, it produces roots that one could link with the ideas of shamanism and earth energies such as crystal healing. The tree trunk grows up into the air and spiritual healing is created, then new branches form and these could be associated with reiki, reconnective healing, and quantum healing. Then new

subbranches and twigs are formed, which could be linked with Sufi reiki, Tera Mai reiki, angelic reiki, sechem reiki, and so on.

Personally, I believe we all unconsciously give healing anyway. For instance, when a child falls over, the parent will "kiss it better." Healing energy is nothing more than the power of love offered unconditionally to a soul to use for its own purpose. Whatever it's called and however it's done, it all stems from the same place, and the closer to source energy we become, then the more powerful the healing becomes, whatever label is given to it. The only way we can get closer to source energy and to the divine within us all, is to heal ourselves of our own issues and problems. We may need to remove blockages, whether they be negative beliefs or early childhood traumas that we have forgotten about but that are still stored in our energy body of chakras and thus in our aura.

Aura Therapies

First, we need to define what we mean by healing. Healing is not curing, and it is not intended to be a cure. A healer connects directly to the universal unconditional love (which they may see as an angel, a deity, a source energy, or something else that they find appropriate), and then the healer channels the energy of unconditional love directly to the person they are working on. That person's soul uses the energy for whatever purpose it chooses for its highest good. The objective of the healer is to be an empty channel for energy rather than to worry about how the energy is used. Healing energy may be used to help a soul pass over, to release blocked energies, or to bring a person back into balance so they can heal themselves.

It is difficult for anyone to heal themselves because we tend to do what we think best, which may not actually be the best. An example would be to keep a pet alive when its soul is saying it's time to go, or trying to treat the symptoms of an illness rather than the cause of the illness itself. Worse still is thinking we know the cause and focusing on treating that instead of letting the energy do what it wants to do—and then being convinced the energy is wrong.

The more we can heal ourselves of past traumas, negative belief patterns, and so on, the clearer our energy body and auras will be. In addition to being healthy, we will also vibrate at a higher energy level, and we will channel higher vibrations to those around us.

How Energy Healing and Aura Therapy Work

Any healer, whatever therapy they are using, will work in one or more of the layers of the aura. A physical therapy such as massage will work on the physical body, but as the therapist moves around, energy will also be going to the aura.

Healing energy in all its forms is used by a subject's soul for their highest good, and while we might want it to effect a cure, that may not be the soul's intention. Some of us have deep-rooted unconscious issues, and on occasion the healing energy received may begin to help, but if someone's consciousness is not ready to move on, then they can and do reject the energy.

Tip

One of the simplest ways of boosting your aura is to change what you're thinking about. Try this as an example:

Think about a memory or something you fear happening, something that makes you sad. Notice how you feel, how you're sitting or standing. Notice what is going on in your body.

Now change what you're thinking about and think about a happy memory or something you're looking forward to. Notice how you're feeling, how you're sitting or standing. Notice what is happening in your body. These changes are reflected in your aura.

You don't have to be a healer to help yourself and others cleanse your aura. After all, everyone needs to start somewhere. We have discussed how imbalances within ourselves are reflected within the aura and chakras, so by using some simple tools and techniques, we can begin the process of clearing and balancing our energy system and thus our lives.

Simple Aura Therapy

At this point I would like to remind you of the section earlier on the importance of your imagination and your unconscious mind (page 43), because if you use your imagination actively, then you will get much better results in the following exercises, which are designed to help cleanse and energize your aura.

EXERCISE 1
FLUFFING

Start by standing. Then, using your hands, fluff your aura up by bending down and starting at your feet and fluffing it all the way up to your head. This is easier to do on someone else than yourself, but it's doable for the self. Do your front and imagine someone else doing your back. Some people use a feather for fluffing. For instance, a Native American shaman would use an eagle feather and usually burn white sage incense as well. An angel reiki practitioner would use a white feather, usually from a swan, and they might also use frankincense essence in a diffuser. This combines fluffing and using the element of fire.

EXERCISE 2
THE ELEMENTS

You can also use any of the natural elements of earth, air, fire, and water in aura therapy. The elements can be used alone or in any combination.

Fire: Light some sage or an incense stick and pass the smoke through your aura using your imagination to see, sense, and feel the smoke cleansing and burning away all negative energy in your aura as it passes through.

Earth: A walk out of doors will refresh and enliven you. You can sit on the ground and imagine all the negative energies in your body and your aura just flowing out through your feet and down into the earth to be transformed back into positive energy.

Air: Imagine the wind blowing through your aura and removing all negative energy and returning it to the universe to be cleansed and turned back into positive energy.

Water: This is the easiest. Whenever you're in the shower, just imagine the water cleansing your aura. As it flows through your aura and over your body, it collects all negative energy taking it down the drain and back to the sea to be transformed into positive energy. Just see, sense, and feel all that gray negativity draining away until the water flowing off you is clean and bright again. Just ask the higher power that is within your personal belief structure—whether that means the divine universal energy, God, individual deities such as Isis or Shiva, angels, or spirit guides—to cleanse and refresh your energy. Imagine divine universal energy coming in through your crown and cleansing, energizing, and balancing each of your chakras, leaving your aura clean and bright.

Protecting Yourself from Energy Leeches

When you're out and about during the day, you pick up negative energy from others unless you know how, to protect your aura, which we will do later. For instance, notice how when you meet someone who is in a bad mood, your mood can change. You end up feeling bad tempered until you throw off their energy or consciously imagine it draining away out of your aura.

If you meet someone who spends an hour moaning at you about something they feel they are helpless to do anything about, you will notice how tired and drained you feel because these people are unconsciously leeching your energy. You can protect yourself from this by simply focusing on your breathing. Imagine you are breathing in universal energy through the top of your head and down to your heart and breathing unconditional love out through your heart. You will feel refreshed and cleansed, and they will automatically receive healing energy without depleting yours.

A MEDITATION TO PROTECT YOUR AURA

There are many meditations and guided visualizations you can buy or download for free from the internet, which you can use to cleanse and protect your aura. You can also create and record them for yourself or just imagine them. The one I give to you here is a general one, which will enable you to not only cleanse your aura and protect it from energy leeches, self-styled victims, and the negative energy of others, but it also begins the process of self-healing by energizing your aura. Wherever there may be blockages within the body's energy system, energy given to the chakras will automatically connect to and clear the auras, because everything is interrelated.

- Relax and make yourself comfortable.
- Focus on your breathing, and with every out-breath, feel yourself becoming more relaxed. Starting with your face, feel the muscles around your eyes, your nose, and your mouth relaxing and releasing tension. Slowly work down your body and feel your neck, shoulders, arms, and hands begin to relax. Feel the tension release from your lower back, your chest, your stomach, and your buttocks. Just let all tension go down through your thighs, calves, feet, and toes while you become totally relaxed.
- Imagine leaving all your problems and worries in a basket at your feet. Then, while feeling your feet firmly on the ground, imagine your feet having roots that reach deep down into the ground, until they connect to divine earth energy, the energy of Mother Earth. Now you feel very safe, secure, and grounded.
- Focus on your in-breath and breathe up the positive energy of Mother Earth. Breathe it up through your feet, calves, thighs, hips, stomach, chest, shoulders, neck, face, and up and out through the top of your head. Imagine the light going up and up into the universe and connecting to the unconditional love of the universe, and breathe that down around your body and down through the top of your head and down through your body and out through your feet and back down to Mother Earth. You are now connected to the earth and universal energy. Just breathe it up and down, and feel it flood through you and around you.

- Imagine the energy beginning to form a hard shell around you, over your head and under your feet, enclosing your aura and protecting it with the pure unconditional loving energy of Mother Earth and Father Universe, and know that nothing can get through it except pure unconditional love.

TIP: Meditation is only limited by your own imagination. One thing that is very easy to do to build on the protective meditation given here is to extend it so that you imagine the white silvery earth energy going up into the universe to connect to the golden universal energy. You can breathe that down into each of your chakras to cleanse and energize them in addition to refreshing and rebalancing your aura.

10 USEFUL TOOLS FOR AURA THERAPY

There are several tools you can use to observe and affect auras. For example, when we enter someone else's auric field their aura and ours will blend, and this can be seen when filmed with aura cameras. An aura spray infused with essential oils can help cleanse or energize the vibration of the aura, as can colors, crystals, and sound. The tool brings its own vibration together with the vibration of the healer who is using it, and so the healer can bring about change in the aura of the person they are working with.

Dowsing

A very simple method to identify and clear blockages from anywhere within the body's energy field is to use a pendulum. Whether you're a trained healer or not, dowsing can help you release blockages without the need to understand the issue causing them. This is often a better way of working, because you can't unconsciously focus the energy on any particular outcome, thus inhibiting the soul's use of the energy.

To do this, all you have to do is program your pendulum to identify and release any blocked energy held within the aura, and you do this by simply asking from the heart.

Slowly pass your pendulum over different parts of the person's body. You can start at the head or the feet. There is no correct or incorrect way to do it—just go with whatever you're drawn to. When the pendulum starts to move and spin, stay with that position until it stops. Then slowly move on until it starts to spin again. By holding your pendulum at different distances away

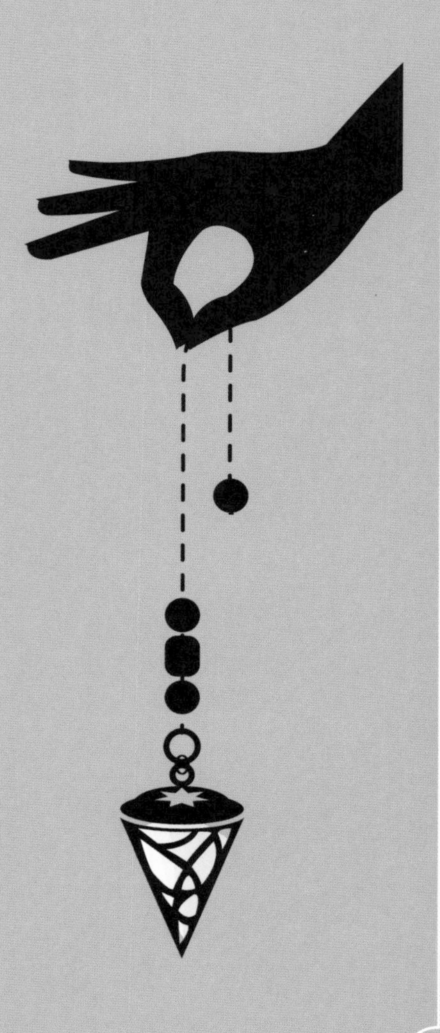

from the body, you will be releasing blockages from each level of the aura. Your pendulum will naturally do this in whichever order is best for yourself or the subject, thus relieving you of the responsibility of *knowing* what you're doing and needing to do it *right.*

Dowsing can also be used as a distance healing technique by using photographs of individuals who need healing. It can even be used to heal relationships by using the pendulum over a photo of the couple. You can also use it to heal a family feud by dowsing over photographs of those involved, because the photo holds the energy of the people's auras, and dowsing can release past issues and bring healing and reconciliation between those concerned.

Color

We have seen that color plays a large part in reflecting our inner and outer energies. The simplest way of adding the color we need is by wearing clothes of that color. When we allow ourselves to choose instinctively what we are going to wear each day, we automatically bring the colors we need into our auras. We also reflect the color of our auras out to the rest of the world. This is something we usually do without thinking every morning as we get dressed. We all have our favorite colors that we wear often, which reflect the main colors of our aura, although there are times when for some reason we choose a completely different color.

By using different-colored cloths or ribbons, we can remove excess color, or more importantly, add healing colors to the aura that are lacking. This is simply done by placing a colored cloth or ribbon or anything of an appropriate color on the physical body for a few minutes or by waving it through the aura. If you haven't got a ribbon, a candle or a piece of fruit or vegetable would also work. Using pendulums made of different-colored crystals is also very effective.

Sound

Sound is another thing that can affect our auras. We all know how music can change the way we feel. Sound is vibration and our auras react to those vibrations. Some music will leave us feeling relaxed and happy, some energized, some angry or just plain uncomfortable. In fact, if you have ever taken a long drive, you have probably had the radio on and deliberately used different types of music to get you through the journey—maybe to relax at first and then you put on something a bit more lively to keep you awake.

There are aura therapies that use sound. These include listening to relaxing music, having a gong bath, drumming, or anything else you fancy.

All parts of the body's energy system and levels of the aura vibrate at differing frequencies and sound is no different. Tibetan singing bowls, cymbals, crystal bowls, gongs, and so on have a variety of tones, and by passing them through the aura, they help release any blocked energy.

Each chakra and auric layer resonates to a different tone. There are also different mantras, be they sounds or words, which resonate with the vibration of each individual layer and chakra. When a sound is tuned into the aura, it then disperses any blockages or smudges within the auric field, clearing them as it goes. If by now you have learned to distinguish the different layers of the aura, then you could tune into each individual layer as well.

Chakra	Auric Layers	Sound	Key
Base	Physical, etheric, causal	Lam	C
Sacral	Etheric, emotional, spiritual	Vam	D
Solar plexus	Emotional, mental	Ram	E
Heart	Upper astral	Yam	F
Throat	Mental, spiritual	Ham	G
Brow	Spiritual, celestial	Om	A
Crown chakra	Celestial, causal	Om	B

Aura Sprays

Another quick and simple way of cleansing and energizing your aura is to use an aura spray, Sprays that you buy in a New Age shop or online can also be used to clear blocked energy from any space and to protect the space, whether it be a home, an office, a venue, or just your special space. Alternatively, you can buy an oil burner or a diffuser that has sticks in a decorative bottle. Oils can be blended by mixing three or more oils together to create specific aromas or a certain vibration. The oils used in store-bought sprays or diffusers may differ, but most will contain lavender, because this has been used as a natural antiseptic since Egyptian times.

There are oils that are recommended for working with specific chakras and with specific layers of the aura, and they can be used alone or with other oils. Use an oil burner or diffusing sticks, because these allow the scent to waft around the room and to be absorbed by all the layers of the aura. It is not a good idea to put essential oils directly onto the skin as they will burn the skin.

The following list shows which essential oils are believed to be best suited to different levels of the aura and connected chakras.

LAYER 1
THE PHYSICAL BODY AND ETHERIC BODIES

Benzoin, patchouli, vetiver, carrot seed, dill, geranium, hyssop, jasmine, marjoram, neroli, rose, sandalwood

This is associated with the base and sacral chakras.

LAYER 2
THE EMOTIONAL BODY

Benzoin, bergamot, black pepper, chamomile, clary sage, cypress, dill, elemi, fennel, hyssop, juniper, lemon, marjoram, neroli, palmarosa, sandalwood, sage

This is associated with the base, sacral, and solar plexus chakras.

LAYER 3
THE MENTAL BODY

Black pepper, clary sage, fennel, lemon, juniper, neroli, bergamot
This is associated with the solar plexus and throat chakras.

LAYER 4
THE ASTRAL BODY

Benzoin, bergamot, cinnamon, clove, elemi, geranium, grapefruit, immortelle, lavender, lime, linden blossom, mandarin, neroli, palmarosa, rose, sandalwood
This is associated with the heart chakra.

LAYER 5
THE SPIRITUAL BODY

Black pepper, blue chamomile, cajeput, cypress, elemi, eucalyptus, myrrh, palmarosa, ravensara, rosemary, sage, yarrow
This is associated with the sacral, throat, and brow chakras.

LAYER 6
THE CELESTIAL BODY

Basil, black pepper, carrot seed, clary sage, clove bud, geranium, ginger, melissa, peppermint, pine, rose, rosemary, rosewood, violet
This is associated with the brow and crown chakras.

LAYER 7
THE CAUSAL LAYER

Frankincense, elemi, jasmine, linden blossom, neroli, rose, rosewood, cedar wood, violet
This is associated with the base and crown chakras.

Warning Do not drink aura sprays, as they could make you ill and are only meant to improve the atmosphere of your surroundings.

Making Your Own Aura Sprays

Depending on what you want to use your spray for, you can use one type of essential oil or a blend to create your own spray. For instance, if you want to cleanse a space, you probably want the spray to smell nice, and blending different cleansing oils together will allow you to create a unique and pleasant scent for this.

If you want to cleanse or invigorate yours or another's aura, then blending the energies of different oils to suit your purpose is necessary. Lavender is a well-known antiseptic and can be used for cleansing spaces as well as auras. It's a versatile oil that can be blended with many others. A blend of lavender and frankincense would cleanse an aura and raise the vibration to gently release blockages from the brow and sacral chakras. If you feel you need to be more grounded, then you could add patchouli or jasmine. In fact, any oil connected to the first layer has grounding properties. Trusting your intuition as you blend oils to an aroma you like will ensure you create the aura spray you need right now.

Warning Do not drink essences, as they could make you ill and are only meant to improve the atmosphere of your surroundings.

To make your own aura spray, add your chosen oil or oils to clean spring water that has been energized by the sun.

The permutations are endless and limited only by your own imagination. There is no right or wrong way to create an aura spray, because they will work as long as your intention is from the heart and as long as you are emotionally connected to the intention.

Tip

You can collect "wild water" from your nearest sacred spring or any natural water source, such as a river, stream, or even freshly gathered rainwater. Good, quality mineral water (not in plastic) is easiest, however, and it is also perfectly suitable.

Essences

Vibrational essences, such as flower essences and crystal elixirs, are more ways of bringing healing energy to the aura. While you can buy essences, you can also make your own.

Making and Using Flower Essences

There are many ways of making essences. For flower essences, select the color or type of flower you want to use. Local species are always best, because they will create a vibrational connection between your own energy (or the energy of the person you want to heal) and your location. Once you have your flowers, wash them. Find a container made from a natural material, such as glass or pottery. In fact, use anything except plastic.

Decide what the essence is going to be used for. For instance, is the intention to remove blocked energy or is it to deliver a boost of energy—or is it both? If it's solely to remove energy, then create the essence over the three days when the moon is full, as this is always a good time to start any clearing or detoxing of the aura. If the essence is intended to boost energy, then do it over the three days of the new moon.

Place your flowers in your clean container. Fill a dark-colored dropper bottle with fresh, glass-bottled mineral water, make sure it is well sealed, and place it in the container with flowers. The day before your selected moon phase, place the container with your flowers and sealed bottle on a windowsill. There, the flowers will be energized by the sun and the moon. The water will absorb the vibrations of the flowers that surround it as well as the energies of the sun and moon.

Your essence is now ready for use. Use the liquid in a diffuser that has special sticks in it that allow the essence to drift around the room or use it in an aura spray. This essence won't keep, so throw away any unused essence after three days and make a fresh batch when needed.

Crystals

Crystals have long been used by as healing tools because of their unique vibrations. Over the centuries, certain crystals have been found to work best for different issues and different illnesses. For instance, moonstone was used by the ancient Egyptians, Greeks, Romans, and druids in fertility rites and is still renowned for that purpose today. For centuries, jade has been considered the stone of wisdom, and turquoise and obsidian have been used for protection.

Over the years, people have continued to discover that different crystals can help heal the body's energy system, whether by wearing a crystal or capturing the vibration in essences and sprays. Crystals help to heal the physical body by raising the vibrations of the wearer's aura. This in turn breaks up dense vibrations that cause blockages by gently releasing past traumas, misassumptions, toxic belief patterns, and anything else that interferes with the energy functions and the transmission of information between the different layers of the aura.

Using Crystals

Individual crystals can be passed through the aura, thus lending their vibration to balance the energies within the aura. Crystal essences can be made exactly like flower essences: by putting crystals in a container and putting a well-sealed, dark-colored stopper bottle filled with fresh mineral water with them. You could also add flowers to the outer container to make a combined crystal and flower essence.

Warning Do not drink crystal essences, as they could make you ill and are only meant to improve the atmosphere of your surroundings.

Crystal vibrations can also be added to aura sprays by first soaking crystals in the water you plan to use prior to blending the water with your chosen oils. The water will absorb the vibrations of the crystals and combine with the oils within the spray.

You can also carry crystals with you, in your pocket or worn as jewelry, to bring their vibrations into your aura. There is no right or wrong way to work with vibrational auric healing therapies, so you need to believe that your

intuition will be your guide. After all, over the years you have probably chosen and worn different jewelry that has brought you the vibrations you needed at the time, and you did this quite unconsciously.

Choosing Crystals

Some crystals are easy to find and inexpensive, whereas others are expensive because of their rarity. Gemstones such as emerald, diamond, and ruby are extremely costly, especially if they have been polished and turned into jewelry. Rubies are said to help ground you and to assist in the manifestation of dreams but are considered unlucky in an engagement ring. Diamonds are the hardest stone, and it is traditional to use them for engagement rings because they are long lasting and contain all the colors of the rainbow when the light catches them.

Most crystals used in healing are those you can easily buy from mind, body, and spirit stores and online. Your intuition as well as the color, shape, and size of the crystals will help you work out what needs to go where—whether you are placing them physically on your body, waving them through the aura, holding them in a particular layer of the aura, or creating an aura spray with them. What follows is an overview of what a variety of crystals can be used for in each layer of the aura.

LAYER 1
THE PHYSICAL AND ETHERIC BODIES

Ruby, garnet, bloodstone, red jasper, black tourmaline, obsidian, smoky quartz

These can all be used for protection, to ground yourself, and to remove dark patches within the aura. The darker the color crystal, the more it can absorb negative energy. These crystals are good for any physical problems relating to "letting go," so they relate to kidneys, colon, legs, knees, hips, and bones. They can be used to help ease diarrhea, which denotes the need to let go of something; constipation, which suggests trying to hold on to something; and illnesses such as IBS and adrenal problems.

LAYER 2
THE EMOTIONAL BODY

Carnelian, coral, gold, calcite, amber, citrine, gold topaz, peach, moonstone, aventurine

These also work in the etheric body, but their focus is on emotional and reproductive issues. They work well with our reproductive organs, bladder, prostate, and spleen and can help with problems around setting boundaries, not feeling good enough, or, in practical terms, problems with fertility.

LAYER 3
THE MENTAL BODY

Citrine, gold topaz, amber, tiger's eye, gold, calcite, selenite, amethyst

This layer represents the center of creativity, so if you are looking for inspiration, then any of the above crystals will do the trick. It is also the layer governing our feelings, so it relates to the pancreas, adrenals, stomach, liver, gallbladder, nervous system, and muscles. The digestive system is responsible for breaking down food and converting it into energy for the healthy functioning of the body, but the spiritual metaphor links it with the way that energy is utilized by the body and how we use energy for our soul's purpose. There is a belief that the liver is where we store anger caused by past hurts, and past hurts can also be reflected as arthritis and the stiffening of the joints as we age. These crystals can help release those hurts.

LAYER 4
THE ASTRAL BODY

Emerald, green and pink tourmaline, malachite, green jade, green aventurine, chrysoprase, kunzite, rose quartz, ruby, obsidian

This level focuses on love, on being able to love ourselves and others unconditionally. It governs our sense of touch, our empathy for others, our relationship to ourselves, and our sense of purpose.

Issues in this layer can manifest in feelings of low self-esteem and being unable to reach out to or touch others. It relates to the heart, thymus gland, circulatory system, arms, hands, and lungs. Issues with any of these parts of the body can be worked on in this layer. Also, the heart is often emotionally fragile, and obsidian worn over the heart as a protection can help break down any barriers there may be to opening the heart to love, which is especially useful after a painful breakup or loss.

LAYER 5
THE SPIRITUAL BODY

Turquoise, chrysocolla, celestite, blue topaz, sodalite, lapis lazuli, aquamarine, azurite, kyanite

This is the level of divine will and of being able to speak and live our truth. It relates to our sense of hearing, thought processes, and ability to communicate our inner truth. Physical problems within the ears such as earache can indicate an infection, but you could also ask yourself if someone is trying to will you to their way of thinking or trying to make you do something that feels wrong to you. Other physical issues of this layer can be related to the thyroid, parathyroid, hypothalamus, throat, mouth, neck, and arms. Maybe someone is being a "pain in the neck," but you can't speak your truth or walk away from them. The positive vibrations can release any blockage and negativity in this layer and bring you back to your center.

ANIMAL THERAPY

Animals have seven layers to their auras just as humans do, and they operate in exactly the same way, so all the therapies that work for people work for animals. In fact, they work better because an animal does not have the same intellectual problems as we humans do. We intellectualize, we don't want to believe, we try to make the healing energy do things that it may not be designed for, or we try to do things that may not be for our highest good. In other words, we allow our thoughts to get in the way. Animals don't do this, and they instinctively know what is good for them. A sickly cat or dog will often just sit at the feet of a natural healer and draw energy from them. They will absorb as much energy as they want, and then get up and walk away.

LAYER 6
THE CELESTIAL BODY

Lapis lazuli, azurite, sodalite, quartz crystal, sapphire, tourmaline, amethyst

When clear of all negativity, we experience the divine qualities of unconditional love and compassion in this layer. It connects to the fourth dimension and to our spiritual guides and deceased loved ones. This is where the intuition that we have developed comes into the fore. It relates to our inner vision and our imaginations. This is the layer that absorbs and appreciates nature, music, art, and everything that is beautiful. Feelings of peace and harmony are found here. When this level is clear of negativity from any other level, it can enhance meditation, inspiration, imagination, and spiritual experiences. Imbalances manifest in the physical body within the pituitary gland, the left eye, and the nose, including the senses of smell and hearing.

LAYER 7
THE CAUSAL BODY

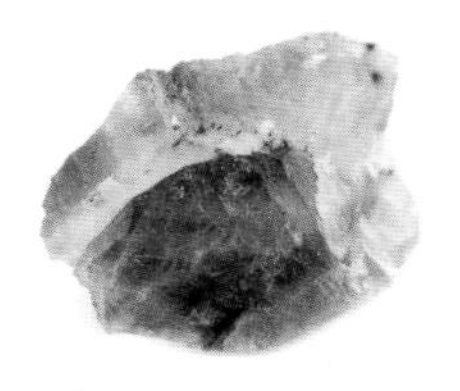

Amethyst, alexandrite, diamond, sugilite, purple fluorite, quartz crystal, selenite

This is the layer where we can experience spiritual bliss, because it connects us to the energy of the universal creator, and it is the layer of enlightenment. It is actually the most resilient layer of them all, and it protects the underlying layers. It is the layer that holds the information about the soul's purpose. It relates to our dreams and the ability to manifest them. Negative energies held in this layer can manifest as problems with the pineal gland, cerebral cortex, central nervous system, and right eye. This is also the layer that focuses the crystal vibrations to the level they need to be to ensure the soul's development.

11

HEALING EACH LAYER OF THE AURA

If you or one of your loved ones becomes sick or depressed, here are some ideas to lift your or their spirits. A useful form of treatment is reiki, because that works directly on the aura, and it reaches down through all seven auric layers. Other forms of energy healing might also be useful. Another good treatment is aromatherapy, because it deals directly with the surface of the body as well as the aura. The use of certain essential oils can help to mend anything that is out of alignment in the auric field.

Here are some quick and easy suggestions for healing each layer of the aura.

LAYER 1
THE PHYSICAL AND ETHERIC BODIES

This is the most physical layer, so it will react badly to discomfort, such as living or working in an uncomfortable environment. If you can't move out of a bad place or have to put up with a difficult job, try the following:

	Meditate while holding a red jasper crystal, as this will help with practical problems.
	Frankincense is a rejuvenating and toning essence, so it helps you cope with difficult surroundings. Use some in a diffuser at home or at work.
♄	Tap into the power of Saturn by wearing dull colors for a while, such as brown, tan, gray, and red ochre.

LAYER 2
THE EMOTIONAL BODY

This is the layer that governs personal feelings, and we all know that people and situations can manage to upset us to the point where we can't think straight. Try the following to ease emotional pain:

	Meditate while holding a carnelian crystal, as this will help with emotional problems.
	Take a bath late in the day and drop in a little mandarin oil as this will have a soothing effect. Also, mandarins are orange and that is a good color for this layer.
☉	Tap into the power of the sun by wearing a peach-colored or orange-colored necklace, scarf, or belt.

LAYER 3
THE MENTAL BODY

It is sometimes difficult to concentrate, especially if there is a lot of noise and activity going on around you, so one solution is to get out into the country or to walk by the sea or a lake and let the busyness of daily life slip away from you for a while. Meanwhile, you can also try the following:

	Meditate while holding a blue stone. Lapis lazuli is fairly stimulating, so use it when you want to put your brain into gear, but if you need to calm down, use blue lace agate.
	Take a bath in the morning using a few drops of melissa oil. This is a citrus-based oil that will stimulate the mental layer of the aura and get your mind working again. Alternatively, use a few drops in a diffuser.
☿	Tap into the power of Mercury by wearing a yellow scarf, belt, or necklace or clothing that is darkish blue for a calming effect—or both!

LAYER 4
THE ASTRAL BODY

This is the bridge between the day-to-day world and the spiritual one, and anyone who is into mind, body, and spirit activities will be familiar with the effects of this layer, because it opens the doors to the subtle realms of imagination and spirituality. If you feel that your creativity has switched itself off or if you are struggling to reach the spiritual world, try the following:

	Meditate using amethyst as this will help you open yourself up to spiritual experiences.
	Put a few drops of patchouli oil into a bath or a diffuser, as it is known to enhance spirituality.
♃	Tap into the power of Jupiter by wearing shades of blue. Jupiter was the king of the Roman gods, so perhaps try royal blue for a while.

LAYER 5
THE SPIRITUAL BODY

Now we leave daily life behind and start to look into matters of belief. If you feel that you have a particular path that you should follow but you feel blocked, either by a shortage of confidence or by people or circumstances, try the following:

	Meditate using tiger's eye, because this helps you tap into your higher will while also grounding you so that you don't lose touch of reality.
	Put a few drops of pine oil into a bath or a diffuser, as it is a combination of spirituality and practicality.
♇	Tap into the power of Pluto, who will help you find inner strength. Do this by wearing something attractive in bright or dark red or shades of purple.

LAYER 6
THE CELESTIAL BODY

Longing for something better can make you desperate to link with your spiritual guides, with angels, or with ancient gods. Whatever you believe, you need to feel better in yourself, and the following can help:

	Meditate using sodalite as it is both spiritual and healing. Sleep with a piece of this crystal on the bedside table.
	Put a few drops of patchouli oil into a bath or a diffuser, as it is known to enhance spirituality.
♀	Tap into the power of Venus, which can help you make links and connections. The traditional colors for this aura layer are pink and green, so wear those shades for a while.

LAYER 7
THE CAUSAL BODY

This layer can link you to the heavenly realms, to angels, spiritual guides, and gods. It can also help you to understand the journey your soul is taking, perhaps by getting a glimpse of your past lives and even of your future path. To tap into this layer, try the following:

	Meditate using a clear crystal as this opens the door to all kinds of possibilities.
	Put a few drops of rosemary oil into a diffuser while meditating. Rosemary has long been known as a sacred plant that can help people understand their soul's purpose.
♆	Tap into the power of Neptune by wearing something lovely in seawater blue and green colors as this will help to connect you to the "other side," especially when meditating with a group of like-minded people.

Coming Back to Earth

Spirituality and journeys of the soul are wonderful, but you still have a life to live, so after working on your aura, close your chakras by imagining them as lights that you turn off. Then put on a pair of comfortable jeans and a brightly colored T-shirt and live your life in the here and now. The bright color will give your aura renewed energy.

AN ANGEL EXERCISE

If you believe in angels, then you will be happy to learn that there are angels who work with each layer of the aura, so asking those specific angels to cleanse the whole aura or to mend a particular layer is another way of clearing the body's energy system of blockages.

Anyone can connect to angels by simply asking for help. You don't need any special rituals, but if you would like to have one, you should create your own. A simple prayer works, but you need to feel the prayer within your heart and allow the outcome to be what it wants to be rather than what you think it should be. You need to trust that the angels will bring you exactly what you need for your highest good and the highest good of anyone else involved.

ACCESSING DIFFERENT DIMENSIONS AND VIBRATIONS

We all have healing and psychic abilities (some more than others), and those abilities are defined by how clear our auras are. Clearing our own energy blockages means that we are more balanced, and happier, and likely to be living a life that is in line with our soul's purpose. The clearer our auras, the higher our vibration will be, and we will be able to channel more healing energy to others and lead a richer and more rewarding life. The higher our vibration, the easier it will be to connect to spirit guides, ascended masters, angels, and deities.

We live in a three-dimensional world and we vibrate to a frequency that is of that dimension. Those who have passed over are believed to reside in the fourth dimension, and thus vibrate at a higher level, which is why we can't see them, although sometimes the image of a dead relative can be seen in someone's aura.

Angels vibrate at a much higher level than those who have passed over; they are said to reside between the fifth and seventh dimensions. Healers and psychics who have spent a lot of time working on themselves by healing and clearing their energy systems can raise their vibration to these dimensions, but you don't have to be a psychic or a healer to ask the angels to cleanse, heal, and revitalize your aura. Anyone can do it simply by asking from the heart.

- This exercise becomes easier and more effective the more you do it.
- Settle yourself comfortably and notice how you feel.
- Say a short prayer from the heart, asking the angels to cleanse and revitalize your aura.
- Notice any changes in the way you feel.
- You will likely feel peaceful and compassionate toward others.

12

HEALING THE AURA AS A WHOLE

As you've learned, the body's energy systems work together, so imbalances in our physical, mental, emotional, or spiritual bodies are reflected throughout the whole system, including all seven layers of the aura. This means that any healing that is carried out on any one level will affect all the levels. There are many different kinds of therapies out there that can help correct imbalances and therefore heal the aura as a whole.

Physical therapies such as Five-Elements Acupuncture work on the physical body by releasing emotional energy blocks within the meridian system. This releases blockages in the chakras and it mends torn or smudged auras. By healing all seven layers of the aura you also heal and realign the physical, emotional, mental, and spiritual bodies. If you focus on healing the chakras, you also heal the aura and the four bodies. Any therapy that is used in any part of the energy system will bring a positive effect to all levels of the aura.

You've seen that the tools you can use for healing the different layers of the aura and chakras include color, aromatherapy oils, crystals, and flower essences as well as dowsing and even food and meal planning. You can also use energy healing methods such as reiki, spiritual healing, crystal healing, and so on. Some aura therapies treat all levels together, or you can focus on one layer or chakra more than another, but the effect is the same. All layers, chakras, and bodies are brought back into alignment by healing the original causes. In this chapter, we're going to explore a few of the healing methods in more depth.

Whatever method you use, it is worth remembering that there are no quick fixes, because healing takes place at the pace that the person's soul demands rather than at the speed we might wish. The patience is worth it, however, because when an issue is found in time, a spot in the aura can be treated, and a potential illness or issue can be averted.

Food and the Aura

Food is a tremendous source of healing. By nourishing your body with healthy food, you are also energizing your auras and your energy system. If you are feeling tired and you sense your aura is dull, then eating a piece of fresh fruit will enliven and brighten your aura. Choosing the right foods for your chakras and aura extends the benefits of aura therapy even after a healing session is over, and it will do so every day because everyone needs to eat.

You can choose foods and colors that aid in the removal of blockages from the chakras, thus healing the physical body and cleansing and repairing the aura at the same time. If you are being blocked from speaking out, you may develop a rip or a dark smudge in your aura that is connected to a blockage in your throat chakra. You could try choosing blue foods, such as blueberries, star flowers, or blue corn to help clear the blockage. Blue foods are not always easy to find, and there aren't a great many of them, but it so happens that the throat chakra works in concert with the solar plexus chakra, so you can also use yellow foods such as eggs, pineapple, spaghetti squash, yellow melons, bananas, and yellow peppers.

We know the heart connects the lower and higher chakras, so you could add green foods such as lettuce and vegetables to your diet, along with medicinal herbs such as rosemary and sage. This can release blocked emotions in those who aren't even aware that they have a problem.

Dark chocolate, avocados, nuts, seeds, and whole grains all contain magnesium, which helps regulate muscle function including maintaining a healthy rhythm. It helps regulate blood pressure and the production of cholesterol. It is also believed to help prevent hearing loss, kidney stones, and migraine headaches, so eating foods that contain magnesium will cleanse all the layers of your aura.

Contracting the Aura

As you know, the seven levels of the aura can expand to several feet (1 m) from a person's body, but this can make working in the aura rather difficult. It's a simple matter to expand or contract your own aura or someone else's. Just visualize a specific layer of the aura expanding to where it is comfortable for you to work with. This is particularly useful if you want to work on one particular layer with a pendulum.

You can also ask all seven layers of the aura to contract to 6 inches (15 cm) from a person's body: Ask the person to breathe the aura in before you work on it. Then place your hands or the pendulum 6 inches (15 cm) from the body, and you will soon find yourself working on all the layers at once.

An Aura Healing Session

If you go to a professional aura healer, a typical session will likely begin with you lying down on a healing couch covered in a multi-colored blanket. Colored crystals are then placed on each of your chakras, and the healer will connect to the healing energy and start to channel it through their hands. They will pass their hands over you at a distance of about 6 inches (15 cm) and their intuition will guide them as to where the blockages or smudges are. The healer might have an imaginary conversation with the smudge by asking what it needs and whether a certain color or essence would help. The healer may pass a colored ribbon through the aura, depending on what is needed. After the session, the healer will likely recommend that you use a diffuser and the essences relevant to your issues to use at home, so the healing can continue there.

Heal Your Own Aura

Here is a simple healing method for your whole aura.

- Start by gathering your tools: aura spray and colored ribbons or crystals that correspond to the layers of the aura.

- Spritz the room you will be healing in with your aura spray.

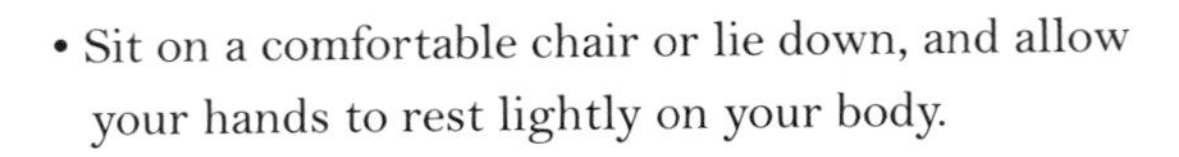

- Sit on a comfortable chair or lie down, and allow your hands to rest lightly on your body.

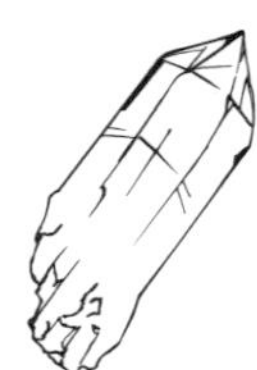

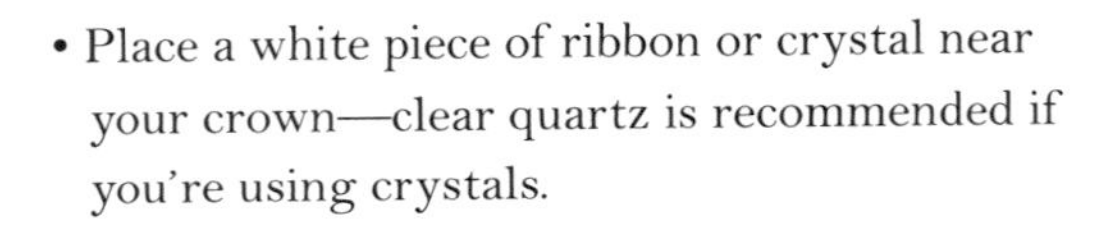

- Place a white piece of ribbon or crystal near your crown—clear quartz is recommended if you're using crystals.

- Then proceed down through the body, placing the appropriate colored ribbon or crystal on or near each chakra as you proceed down the body

- Breathe in so that your aura shrinks back to no more than 6 inches (15 cm) that surround your body.

- Continue to focus on your breath, and imagine that you're breathing in pure golden-silver light of universal loving and healing energy, and that you're breathing it out through your head into your crown chakra.

- Visualize the energy going into your crown and out through all layers of your aura. When you get to your body, visualize the energy flowing through you, from the crown chakra, and down through each chakra. When you reach the base chakra continue through the hips, knees, and feet and then work your way back up the body back to your head.

- Give yourself a moment to come back to awareness of the outside world.

How to Calm Your Aura in a Stressful Situation

This is a good meditation for those occasions when you may feel that you can't do whatever is being asked of you. If you are religious or have an affinity to a deity or an angel, you can pray to them to help you with this exercise.

- Sit comfortably, close your eyes, and focus on your breathing. As you breathe gently in and out, say to yourself, "I am breathing in peace and love and breathing out all stress and negativity."

- Imagine as you breathe that you are breathing in the colors of peace and love, which are pink, pale green, or pale blue. With each outward breath, visualize and feel all the negative gray energy leaving your body and your aura as you become relaxed and calm.

- Feel the gentle rise and fall of your chest as you gently breathe in the colors of peace and love, and breathe out your worries and fears.

- As you breathe, be aware of how your aura is becoming brighter and lighter and how you are feeling at peace with yourself.

- Keep breathing like this for a minute or two as you repeat to yourself, "I am calm and relaxed. I am calm and relaxed. I am calm and relaxed."

- Once you feel calm and relaxed, say, "I am guided by [use the name of your chosen deity or your own inner wisdom]." Repeat that mantra twice more.

- Now say to yourself, "I can do this, I can do this, I can do this."

- When you are ready, slowly open your eyes, sit or stand up straight, and tune back in to your surroundings.

Healing Energy

Whether you call healing energy "spiritual healing" or "reiki," you are working with universal energy, and it is something that comes from the heart. If you work as a healer, you are connecting to the energy via your heart, via your feelings of unconditional love and compassion for your client, or for yourself if you need to heal yourself. But you don't have to be formally trained in any specific school of healing to channel healing energy, because it's something we can all do. Training gives you the opportunity to practice, but there is no right or wrong way to heal, nor is one form of healing stronger or better than another. The vibration can only be as high as the channel is clear. If you have a religious affiliation, you can pray and ask for the help and intercession of whichever deity you feel most connected to. You can create your own ritual for this, or a simple prayer will do just as well.

Healing is a gentle process that can take many sessions to complete, although you should see improvement within the first three to six sessions. The soul is careful not to pass more energy than a person can deal with at any one time.

EXERCISE FOR CONNECTING TO HEALING ENERGY

This is the simplest way of connecting to healing energy, and the meditation in itself is a self-healing meditation. It is also the foundation of further meditations that can be used for healing and balancing all the chakras and all the layers of the aura.

- Sit comfortably and take three deep breaths to center and ground yourself.

- When you are ready, ask your deity or inner wisdom to connect you to universal healing energy.

- Rub your hands together vigorously for a minute until you feel them getting warm. Now hold your hands about 12 to 18 inches (30 to 45 cm) apart.

- Focus on your breathing; imagine you are breathing in universal healing energy. Feel that energy surrounding you. As you breathe out, imagine the energy coming out through your hands.

- You may feel a light tingling sensation in your hands, but if you don't, it doesn't matter because the healing will still work. Just keep breathing the energy in and breathing it out through your hands.

- Then move your hands anywhere in your aura and start sending that healing energy wherever you feel needs it.

GUIDED VISUALIZATION TO A CRYSTAL HEALING POOL

This final guided meditation will help you heal yourself physically and emotionally if the need arises.

In this exercise you will be taking a journey to the crystal temple of healing, where you will immerse yourself in the pool of life and heal your soul self.

- Start by sitting comfortably. Focus on your breathing.
- Imagine your feet have roots that reach deep down into the ground until they connect to divine earth energy, the energy of Mother Earth. Embrace the feelings of safety, security, and being grounded.
- Now, through your roots, breathe that energy up, opening your chakras one by one, and then coming out of your crown chakra and connecting you to the golden universal energy.
- Feel that you are fully open and protected.

- Now, imagine yourself floating out into the universe along that golden thread of universal energy. You are being taken to a crystal temple where all the healers of the universe congregate under the direction of the throne of Archangel Raphael, the angel of healing.
- As you enter the temple, you are led to a crystal cave. It is made of whatever type of crystal in whatever color you need right now.
- In the middle of the cave is a gentle waterfall of crystal-clear water that falls into a pool, which is as deep as you wish it to be. Surrounding the pool are angels, ascended masters, and all the healers of the universe as well as all those who love you.
- Enter the water and make your way to the waterfall. Notice the unconditional loving energy in which all the healers are holding you. Stand under the waterfall and feel the water of life cleanse and revitalize all the layers of your aura.
- Take a cup and drink the water from the waterfall. Feel the water going through your body. Notice all the dark smudgy issues leaving your body as your aura is transformed back into crystal-clear water. Ask that the healing go backward across time to heal any past life traumas as well.
- Stay under the waterfall and in the pool for as long as you wish. Know that you can return to this place at any time in the future just by remembering this visualization.
- When you are ready, thank all the healers, angels, and loved ones for the healing you have received, and make your way back across the universe, following the golden thread, back into your body.
- Close your chakras one by one, breathe up your roots, and slowly open your eyes.

CONCLUSION

Aura reading is not an easy subject to master, but this book should help you understand the link between the layers of the aura and the link between the aura and the chakras. If you practice seeing auras, your ability will grow, and with this book to refer back to, you can check out the colors that you see and interpret them for yourself.

Don't worry if you are getting on in years. Many psychic people only develop their skills later in life, once they have got past the business of working hard and bringing up a family. Having a bit of experience behind you can only help! So enjoy your aura experience and live as good and happy a life as you possibly can.

Good luck,
Joylina

ABOUT THE AUTHOR

Joylina is an inspirational speaker, life coach, counselor, angel expert, psychic clairvoyant, healer, teacher, and author. She gave up a career in professional services marketing in 2000 so that she could use her life-coaching and counseling skills. She has been a reiki master since 1997. She set out to help people with their personal and spiritual development and to enable them to live happy, healthy, and rewarding lives. She has written three books, including the acclaimed *Your Angel Journey*. The two others are about psychic development and the tarot and are in the process of being published by Zambezi Publishing Ltd.

Joylina was president of the British Astrological and Psychic Society and was responsible for creating and updating many of their courses as well as assessing new members. She is now a consultant member of MBS Professionals Ltd. She avidly believes in maintaining high ethical standards and integrity within her chosen field of personal and spiritual development and all things related to mind, body, and spirit. She has taught at the College of Psychic Studies in London as well as traveled to many spiritual energy spots around the world, leading spiritual workshops and retreats.

Currently she focuses on writing and developing her own line of training courses while also caring for her parents and grandchildren. She lives in the southwest of England and enjoys walking her dogs along the beautiful Jurassic Coast that she has made her home.

INDEX

IMAGE CREDITS

Cover: frame © painterr/Shutterstock; human figure© DeoSum/Shutterstock; burst © Peratek/ Shutterstock; background texture © Andrius_Saz/Shutterstock

Poster: frame © painterr/Shutterstock, background texture © Andrius_Saz/Shutterstock, aura figure © DeoSum/Shutterstock, chakra symbols by Terry Marks

Interior: right (r), left (l), top (t), bottom (b), middle (m)

Images provided by the author: 52, 53
Illustrations by Terry Marks: 21, 22, 23, 24, 36, 99, 129; symbols on 120, 121, 122, 123
Image by Sérgio Valle Duarte (used without adaptation under creativecommons.org/licenses/ by/4.0/deed.en): 10

Shutterstock: 9 © drawhunter; 14, 15, 16, 17 © Olga Guitere; 19, 72, 73, 74, 75, 76, 77, 78, 79, 80 © DeoSum; 25 © Baleika Tamara; 26 © umnola; 30, 33, 34 (icon), 36 (icon), 39 © A Aleksii; 31 © eveleen; 34 © Morphart Creation; 35 © aninata; 37, 112, 130 (b) © dariatroi; 40 © EngravingFactory; 43 © intueri; 45, 125 © Gorbash Varvara; 46 © 3Dimka; 47 © Benjavisa Ruangvaree Art; 48 © Elchin Jafarli; 49 (l) © revoltan; 49 (r) © Pani Lena; 56 © Galyna_P; 57 © Alhovik; 59 © xpixel; 83 © TopStudio; 84 © mart; 97 © provector; 100 © Peratek; 101 © anttoniart; 103 © NatBasil; 105 © Mercury Green; 108 (b), 123 (herb), 130 (l) © Bodor Tivadar; 108 (icon) © Sir.Vector; 108, 109, 120 (herbs), 121 (herbs), 122 (herbs) © Foxyliam; 109 (b) © Volkova Anna; 109 (m) © Epine; 111 © logaryphmic; 113 © Nikki Zalewski; 114 (b) © ntv; 114 (t) © aregfly; 115 (b), 121 (lapis lazuli), 122 (tiger's eye), 123 (crystal) © vvoe; 115 (t) © Anastasia Bulanova; 116 © hadkhanong; 117 (t) © Ademoeller; 117, 114 (m), 120 (carnelian) © Coldmoon Photoproject; 119 © SvetaZi; 120 (jasper) © Ilizia; 121 (amethyst) © Jirik V; 122 (sodalite) © Nastya22; 128 (b) © adehoidar; 128 (m) P© aintDoor; 128 (t) © Kaidash; 130 (r) © Nats Garu; 133 © QueenAnn5; 134 © Space Oleandr; 136 © Reamolko; chapter opener bursts © Peratek